The **MAILBOX** ® The Education Center®

LANGUAGE ARTS
INDEPENDENT PRACTICE

grade **1**

SUPER SIMPLE!

 **144**

EASY-TO-USE IDE[AS]
SKILL REINFORCE[...]

 ✓ Phonemic awareness

 ✓ Vocabulary

✓ Phonics

 ✓ High-frequency words

✓ Reading comprehension

 ✓ Writing

✓ Spelling

 ✓ **AND LOTS MORE!**

ENOUGH FOR
4 activities for every week
OF THE SCHOOL YEAR

Managing Editors: Gerri Primak and Kelly Robertson

Editorial Team: Stephanie Affinito, Becky S. Andrews, Randi Austin, Diane Badden, Erica Bohrer, Kimberley Bruck, Karen A. Brudnak, Kitty Campbell, Jenny Chapman, Chris Curry, Jill Davis, Stacie Stone Davis, Lynette Dickerson, Jennifer Feldman, Kristin Bauer Ganoung, Deborah Garmon, Kathy Ginn, Pam Girgenti, Theresa Lewis Goode, Ada Goren, Heather Graley, Tazmen Hansen, Marsha Heim, Lori Z. Henry, Sherry Hull, Debra Liverman, Dorothy C. McKinney, Thad H. McLaurin, Carolyn Mikelson, Lisa Mountcasel, Sharon Murphy, Jennifer Nunn, Mark Rainey, Jan Robbins, Hope Rodgers, Rebecca Saunders, Betty Silkunas, Andrea Singleton, Barry Slate, Zane Williard, Joyce Wilson, Katie Zuehlke

www.themailbox.com

©2008 The Mailbox® Books
All rights reserved.
ISBN10 #1-56234-839-6 • ISBN13 #978-156234-839-7

Manufactured in the United States
10 9 8 7 6 5 4 3 2 1

Table of Contents

Set 1 ....**4**
- [ ] letter formation
- [ ] alphabetical order
- [ ] name spelling
- [ ] beginning sounds

Set 2 ....**6**
- [ ] word families
- [ ] writing sentences
- [ ] syllables
- [ ] high-frequency words

Set 3 ....**8**
- [ ] letter formation
- [ ] writing sentences
- [ ] beginning sounds
- [ ] capitalization

Set 4 .... **10**
- [ ] word families
- [ ] sorting words
- [ ] beginning sounds
- [ ] high-frequency words

Set 5 .... **12**
- [ ] vowel identification
- [ ] rhyming
- [ ] writing
- [ ] nouns

Set 6 .... **14**
- [ ] initial consonants
- [ ] word families
- [ ] spelling
- [ ] descriptive writing

Set 7 .... **16**
- [ ] capitalization
- [ ] short vowels
- [ ] sorting words
- [ ] high-frequency words

Set 8 .... **18**
- [ ] high-frequency words
- [ ] punctuation
- [ ] spelling
- [ ] spelling CVC words

Set 9 ....**20**
- [ ] initial consonants
- [ ] rhyming
- [ ] making words
- [ ] making predictions

Set 10 ....**22**
- [ ] recalling story parts
- [ ] creative writing
- [ ] short-vowel sounds
- [ ] high-frequency words

Set 11 ....**24**
- [ ] fantasy and reality
- [ ] character analysis
- [ ] beginning letters *c, h, p, t*
- [ ] word families

Set 12 ....**26**
- [ ] spelling CVC words
- [ ] sorting words
- [ ] alphabetical order
- [ ] word wall words

Set 13 ....**28**
- [ ] beginning sounds
- [ ] writing sentences
- [ ] punctuation
- [ ] literary response

Set 14 ....**30**
- [ ] punctuation
- [ ] nouns
- [ ] sorting words
- [ ] syllables

Set 15 ....**32**
- [ ] capitalization
- [ ] short vowels
- [ ] word families
- [ ] comparing characters

Set 16 ....**34**
- [ ] initial consonants
- [ ] writing a caption
- [ ] retelling a story
- [ ] alphabetical order

Set 17 ....**36**
- [ ] purpose for reading
- [ ] writing sentences
- [ ] initial consonants
- [ ] literary response

Set 18 ....**38**
- [ ] editing sentences
- [ ] cause and effect
- [ ] ending sounds
- [ ] writing a list

To use the table of contents as a checklist, make a copy of pages 2 and 3. Staple or clip each copy on top of its original page. Each time you use an activity, check its box. Start each school year with fresh copies of the pages.

Skills Index on pages 111-112.

Set 19 40
- [ ] literary response
- [ ] onsets and rimes
- [ ] nouns
- [ ] segmenting words

Set 20 42
- [ ] syllables
- [ ] writing
- [ ] word families
- [ ] synonyms

Set 21 44
- [ ] compound words
- [ ] verbs
- [ ] literary response
- [ ] writing ideas

Set 22 46
- [ ] short-vowel o
- [ ] spelling
- [ ] plural nouns
- [ ] sentence subjects

Set 23 48
- [ ] main idea and details
- [ ] final consonants
- [ ] beginning blends
- [ ] onsets and rimes

Set 24 50
- [ ] nouns
- [ ] compound words
- [ ] author's purpose
- [ ] contractions

Set 25 52
- [ ] long vowels
- [ ] writing organization
- [ ] short vowels
- [ ] antonyms

Set 26 54
- [ ] synonyms
- [ ] subject-verb agreement
- [ ] sorting words
- [ ] writing a story

Set 27 56
- [ ] word families
- [ ] word wall words
- [ ] compound words
- [ ] plurals

Set 28 58
- [ ] final consonants
- [ ] writing sentences
- [ ] writing directions
- [ ] literary response

Set 29 60
- [ ] beginning blends
- [ ] verbs
- [ ] plurals
- [ ] writing a list

Set 30 62
- [ ] literary response
- [ ] sounds of c and g
- [ ] consonant digraphs
- [ ] adjectives

Set 31 64
- [ ] high-frequency words
- [ ] long and short vowels
- [ ] nouns and verbs
- [ ] antonyms

Set 32 66
- [ ] word families
- [ ] contractions
- [ ] r-controlled vowels
- [ ] cause and effect

Set 33 68
- [ ] writing a list
- [ ] facts from nonfiction
- [ ] long and short vowels
- [ ] high-frequency words

Set 34 70
- [ ] creative writing
- [ ] consonant digraphs
- [ ] CVCe spelling pattern
- [ ] inflectional endings

Set 35 72
- [ ] alphabetical order
- [ ] adjectives
- [ ] parts of speech
- [ ] comprehension

Set 36 74
- [ ] writing a letter
- [ ] contractions
- [ ] plurals
- [ ] making connections

Letter Sculptures

Letter formation

Materials:
uppercase and lowercase letter cards
play dough

A child chooses a letter card. He molds the play dough to form the uppercase and lowercase letters shown on the card. When he is satisfied with his work, he chooses a different card and repeats the activity.

Orderly Shapes

Alphabetical order

Materials:
26 die-cut shapes, each labeled with
    a different letter
alphabet chart

A student randomly takes five shapes and names the letter on each shape. Then she puts the shapes in alphabetical order. She uses the alphabet chart to check her work. To repeat the activity, she returns the shapes to the original pile, takes five more shapes, and orders them.

Letter by Letter

Name spelling

Materials:
set of letter cards
12" x 18" sheets of construction
    paper (one per child)

A youngster writes on a sheet of paper a blank for each letter of her name. Then she takes a letter card and determines whether the letter is in her name. If it is, she writes the letter on each corresponding blank, making sure to capitalize the first letter of her name. If the letter is not in her name, she sets the card aside. She continues until she has correctly spelled her name.

Sounds the Same

Beginning sounds

Materials:
student copies of a recording sheet,
    similar to the one shown
magazines
scissors
glue

A student writes her name on a recording sheet. She quietly says her name aloud, stressing the beginning sound. Then she cuts out magazine pictures that have the same beginning sound as her name. She glues each picture on the page.

Is It a Word?

Word families

Materials:
rime card labeled -*at*
letter tiles: *b, c, d, h, l, m, s, z*
blank paper
crayons

A student makes a T chart on blank paper. She labels one column with a happy face and the other with a sad face. Next, she places one onset (letter tile) beside the rime card. If the two make a real word, she writes the word below the happy face. If they do not, she writes the nonsense word below the sad face. She uses each remaining onset to build and write a real or nonsense word.

☺	☹
cat	lat
hat	dat
mat	zat
bat	
sat	

Teta

Tell About It

Writing sentences

Materials:
box with a lid
items to put in the box (such as a key, clean sock, spoon, or shell)
writing paper
crayons

A youngster removes one item from the box and draws it on his paper. He writes a sentence that names the item and tells about it. Then he returns the item to the box. He chooses a different item and repeats the activity.

Chris

The shell is pretty.

The sock is big.

Tap, Tap, Tap

Syllables

Materials:
student copies of the picture cards on page 76
scissors

A student names the picture on each card and uses his hand to quietly tap out each part, or syllable, in the word. For each word part he hears, he colors one dot at the bottom of the card. Then he colors the pictures, cuts out the cards, and stacks the cards in a neat pile. At an appropriate time, he asks to have his stack of cards stapled at the top.

Truck Stop

High-frequency words

Materials:
student copies of the word cards on page 76
6" x 12" paper strips (one per child)
alphabet letter stampers
ink pad
scissors
glue
crayons

A child cuts out a high-frequency word card. He glues the card to the left edge of a paper strip. He says the word. Next, he names each letter in the word as he stamps the letter on the paper strip. Then he reads the word and writes it on the strip. He draws a rectangle around his work, which becomes the trailer for the truck. Then he continues to read and spell the high-frequency word as he adds wheels and other truck-related details to the project.

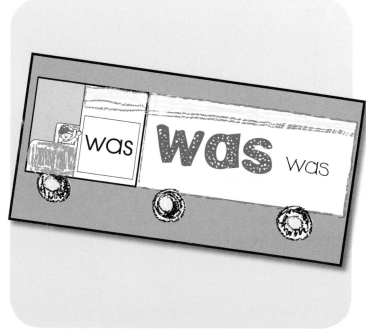

Buried Letters

Letter formation

Materials:
letter manipulatives buried in a tub of sand
writing paper
highlighter

A student removes a letter from the tub. He traces the letter with his finger and then uses his best handwriting to copy it on his paper five times. He examines his work and uses the highlighter to circle his neatest example. He sets the letter aside and continues in the same manner until he has found and copied a predetermined number of letters.

Sentences From Stamps

Writing sentences

Materials:
variety of picture stampers
ink pad
writing paper

A youngster stamps pictures at the top of her paper. Then she writes a sentence about each object she stamped. For an added challenge, the child writes a story that incorporates all the stamped pictures.

Pairs of Socks

Beginning sounds

Materials:
student copies of page 77
envelopes (one per child)
crayons
scissors

A student decorates an envelope to resemble a clothes dryer and cuts out a set of picture cards. She pairs the cards by beginning sounds. Then she puts them in the clothes dryer to take home for additional practice.

Clip It!

Capitalizing a sentence

Materials:
sentence strips labeled with sentences, some without initial capital letters
capital letter cards that correspond with the first letter of each sentence
clothespins

A child reads a sentence. If it needs a capital letter, he uses a clothespin to clip the corresponding letter card in place. If it does not need a capital letter, he sets the sentence aside. He continues in this manner until all the sentences are correctly capitalized.

Sort It Out

Word families

Materials:
4 cards labeled with *-an* words
4 cards labeled with *-at* words
blank paper

A student divides each of two sheets of paper into four sections. She reads the word cards and sorts them by word family. She writes each group of words on a separate sheet of paper, writing one word in each section. Then she illustrates each word.

Number or Color?

Sorting words by category

Materials:
2 paper plates labeled as shown
cards labeled with number and color words
blank paper

A student takes a card and reads the word. He determines whether it is a number or a color and places it on the appropriate plate. He continues in this manner until each card has been sorted. For an added challenge, the child copies the number words on a blank sheet of paper and writes the corresponding numeral beside each word. Then he copies the color words onto the paper and colors a small corresponding colored circle beside each word.

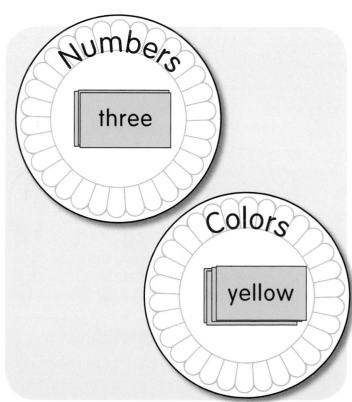

Finding Pairs

Beginning sounds

Materials:
magazines
12" x 18" sheets of construction paper (one per child)
scissors
glue
marker

A child finds in a magazine a pair of pictures that begin with the same sound. He cuts out the pictures. Next, he glues the pictures on a sheet of construction paper, draws a ring around them, and writes the corresponding beginning sound in the ring. He continues in the same manner until he has found four sets of pictures.

Hopscotch Fun

High-frequency words

Materials:
student copies of page 78, labeled with high-frequency words
cotton ball

For a variation on the game of hopscotch, a child tosses a cotton ball onto a square on a hopscotch grid. Beginning with the first square, he quietly reads each word aloud until he reaches the cotton ball. If the cotton ball lands outside the grid, he reads each word on the grid aloud. He continues in the same manner as time allows.

Hunt and Highlight

Vowel identification

Materials:
small whiteboard, labeled as shown
newspaper pages
construction paper (one sheet per child)
dry-erase marker
eraser
highlighter
scissors
glue

A student cuts out five words in large print from the newspaper and highlights the vowels in each word. He glues each word on a sheet of construction paper. Then he counts and makes a tally mark on the whiteboard for each high-lighted vowel. When he's satisfied with his work, he erases the tally marks.

Memory Matchup

Rhyming

Materials:
construction paper copy of page 79, cut apart
blank paper
pocket chart

A youngster shuffles the cards and places them facedown in columns in a pocket chart. He searches for a rhyming pair by randomly turning over two cards. If the two cards do not match, he turns them back over and flips two new cards. When he locates a rhyming pair, he removes the cards and writes the two words side by side on his paper. He continues playing until all the rhyming pairs have been found.

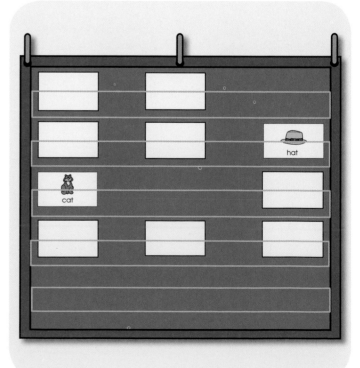

Simple Story

Writing

Materials:
student copies of the sentence starter
    strips on page 82
construction paper (one sheet per child)
blank paper (four sheets per child)
scissors
glue
crayons

A child writes endings to the four sentence starters to create a simple story. She cuts the strips apart and glues each one on a separate sheet of paper. Then she puts the pages in order and adds illustrations, a cover, and a title to create a book. At an appropriate time, she asks to have her booklet pages stapled together.

Nursery Rhyme Time

Nouns

Materials:
story paper
poster of a familiar nursery rhyme with
    the nouns underlined

A student reads the posted nursery rhyme. She rewrites the rhyme, changing each underlined word or phrase to a new naming word or phrase. Then she adds an illustration.

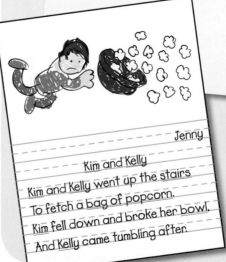

Lift a Letter

Initial consonants

Materials:
blank cards (four per child)
blank paper
tape
crayons

A student writes a consonant on each of four cards and tapes the top of each card to a sheet of paper. Then she lifts each card and draws a picture underneath that begins with the corresponding letter. For an added challenge, the child labels each picture.

Piece by Piece

Word families

Materials:
construction paper word family puzzle like the one shown
3 additional puzzle shapes, each labeled with a word not in the featured word family

A child spreads out the pieces of the puzzle and locates the word family piece. He reads the word on each remaining piece and places it with the word family piece if it belongs. He then assembles the puzzle to check whether his sorting is correct.

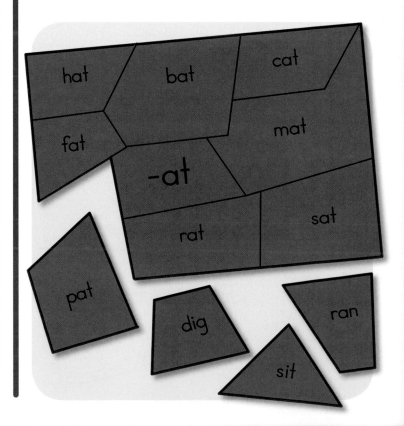

Spelling Bee

Spelling

Materials:
yellow construction paper ovals (one per student)
word cards with a correct and incorrect spelling on each

A youngster decorates a yellow oval to make a very simple bee. He looks at the words on a card and turns the correct side faceup, and stacks the cards in a pile. He then writes the correctly spelled words on the back of his bee cutout.

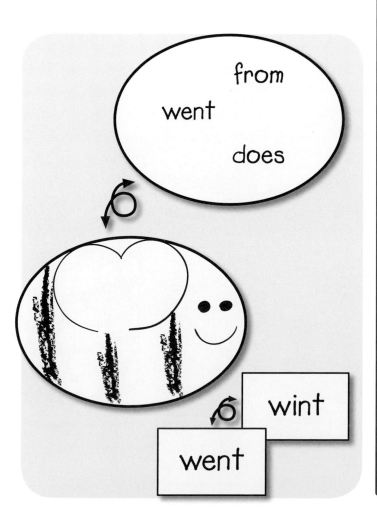

Weave a Web

Descriptive writing

Materials:
cards labeled with nouns
blank paper

A student reads the noun on a card. She draws and labels a picture of the noun in the center of her paper. From the picture, she draws four or five lines with circles at the ends. Inside each of these circles, she writes a word that describes the noun. For an added challenge, the youngster uses the descriptive words to write on the back of her paper one or more sentences about the noun.

Capital Drive

Capitalization

Materials:
small toy car
sentence strips labeled with sentences
    with incorrect capitalization
writing paper

A student places a sentence strip (Capital Drive) on a flat surface. He "drives" his car down Capital Drive, stopping when he sees a word that needs a capital letter. Then he writes the sentence correctly onto his paper and repeats the process with a different sentence strip.

Say and Sort

Short vowels

Materials:
student copies of page 80
box, labeled as shown
gift bag, labeled as shown
mug, labeled as shown
scissors

A child cuts out the cards and arranges them faceup. For each card, she identifies which container (the box, bag, or mug) has the matching vowel sound and then places the card in that container. For an added challenge, the student writes the corresponding word on the back of each card.

Shoe Sort

Sorting words by category

Materials:
copy of page 81, cut apart
four empty shoeboxes, labeled as shown
blank paper

A youngster reads the word on a card. She determines which category the word belongs to and places the card in the corresponding box. Once all the cards have been sorted, she makes a four-column chart on her paper and labels each column with a different category. Then she writes each word in the correct column.

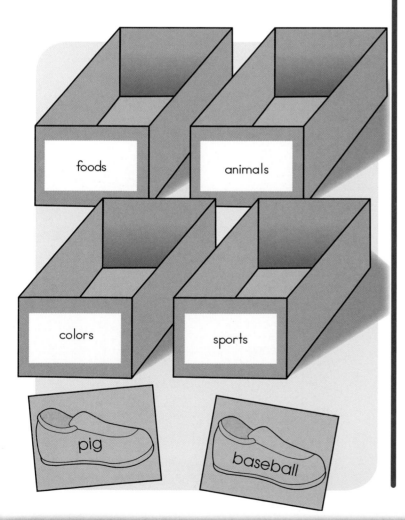

In the News

High-frequency words

Materials:
take-out menus, newspaper articles, magazine pages (enough for several per student)
list of high-frequency words
writing paper
highlighters

A student selects a newspaper article, menu, or magazine page. Then he searches the text for the words from the list. When he locates a word, he highlights it and records it on his paper. If time allows, he selects a different piece of text to search again.

Food Find

High-frequency words

Materials:
clean, empty food boxes and containers
blank paper
list of high-frequency words

A youngster reviews the list of high-frequency words. He searches a food container for the listed words. When he finds a word, he writes it on his paper. If he finds the same word more than once, he makes a tally mark after the word on his paper. He continues searching the food containers until he has found each word at least once.

Come to a Stop

Punctuation

Materials:
sentence strips, each labeled with a statement or question without ending punctuation
small paper stop sign labeled with a period on one side and a question mark on the other
writing paper

A child reads a sentence and places the stop sign with the correct punctuation mark faceup at the end. Then he copies the sentence onto a sheet of paper. He continues in this manner with each remaining sentence.

String Along

Spelling

Materials:
yarn cut into various lengths

A student chooses a word from the word wall and uses lengths of yarn to form the letters. Then she spells the word again, this time without looking at the spelling. Once she is satisfied with her spelling, she looks at the word wall to check her work.

Making Words

Spelling CVC words

Materials:
copy of the vowel spinner on page 82, prepared as shown
cards programmed with CVC words, replacing the vowel in each word with a blank
blank paper

A student folds a sheet of paper into eight sections as shown. Then she takes a card and spins the spinner. If adding the vowel to the consonants makes a word, she writes the word in a section of her paper. If adding the vowel does not make a word, she spins again until a word can be made. She continues until each section of her paper contains a word.

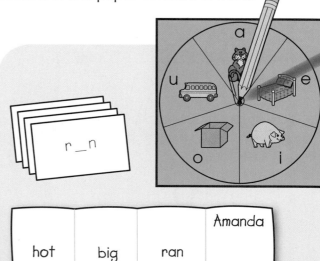

Find Four

Initial consonants

Materials:
6–8 objects (four that begin with the same letter)
blank paper
crayons

A student names each object, stressing the beginning sound. He finds the four objects that begin with the same letter and then writes the corresponding letter in the center of a sheet of paper. He draws a picture of each item that begins with the letter in a separate corner of the paper and then labels each picture.

Flipping Flapjacks

Rhyming

Materials:
tagboard copies of page 83 (one per child)
spatula
scissors
crayons

A youngster cuts out the flapjacks. He reads the word on a flapjack and uses the spatula to flip it over. He writes a rhyming word on the blank side and then draws a matching picture. He repeats the activity with the remaining flapjacks.

Alphabet Soup

Making words

Materials:
letter manipulatives in a soup pot
ladle
writing paper

A child uses the ladle to scoop several letters out of the pot. She uses some or all of the selected letters to form a word and then writes it on her paper. (If a word cannot be made, she takes another scoop of letters.) She rearranges the letters to form additional words and adds them to her list. Then she returns the letters to the pot. She takes additional scoops of letters and forms words as time allows.

RACK

Tamara

ran
car
net
can
rack

What's in a Title?

Making predictions

Materials:
unfamiliar book title written on the board
story paper

A youngster reads the book title. Then she draws a picture of something she predicts might happen in the book and writes a sentence about her picture. After each student has completed the activity, read the book aloud and allow children to compare their predictions with what actually happens in the story.

Monster Pet!

Emma

I think that this story will be about a kid who has a monster as a pet.

Triangular Retelling

Recalling the parts of a story

Materials:
three 4" x 6" cards
tape
several previously read books

A youngster chooses a book to review. Then she writes a sentence describing the beginning, middle, and end of the story on separate cards. She tapes the cards together, in order, and then tapes the first card to the third card to make a triangular prism. To retell the story, she starts with the first card and then flips the prism as needed.

In the beginning, Arthur is upset because he got a strict teacher.

In the middle, Arthur studies hard.

In the end, Arthur wins the spelling bee.

Describing a Doodle

Creative writing

Materials:
story paper
black marker
crayons

A child uses the marker to draw a doodle at the top of his paper. He incorporates the doodle into an illustration. Then he writes a sentence or two describing his picture.

The boy has cool sunglasses. They are big and cover his whole face.

Kevin

Spin a Vowel

Short-vowel sounds

Materials:
copy of the vowel spinner on page 82, prepared
  as shown
blank paper
crayons

A child makes a recording sheet similar to the one shown. Then she spins the spinner. She identifies an object that has the same short-vowel sound as indicated on the spinner and then draws it in a corresponding space on her recording sheet. If the spaces are full, she spins the spinner again until it lands on a different vowel. She continues in this manner until her recording sheet is completed.

Searching for Words

High-frequency words

Materials:
list of high-frequency words
sticky notes
familiar book

A student makes a T chart on a sticky note. He chooses two high-frequency words from the list and writes them on his sticky note as shown. Then he reads the book, looking for the two words as he reads. When he finds a word, he makes a tally mark beneath the word on his sticky note. After reading the book, he totals the tally marks.

Could It Happen?

Fantasy and reality

Materials:
student copies of page 84
construction paper (two sheets per child)
crayons
scissors
glue

A student labels the sheets of construction paper as shown. After he colors and cuts out the picture cards, he takes a card and determines if the event pictured is fantasy or reality. Then he glues the card on the appropriate sheet of construction paper. He continues in this manner until each card has been sorted.

From Beginning to End

Character analysis

Materials:
several books with easily identifiable main characters
blank paper
crayons

A child folds a sheet of paper in half and then unfolds it. She chooses a book and writes the name of the main character across the top of her paper. Then she labels her paper as shown. She writes a sentence describing the character at the beginning of the book and at the end of the book on the appropriate sides of her paper and then adds illustrations.

Lilly

Beginning — She wants her way and wants everyone to see her purse.

End — She learns to wait to share.

LaKeisha

What a Spread!

Beginning letters c, h, p, t

Materials:
copy of page 85, cut apart
four paper plates, labeled as shown

A child says the name of each food item, stressing the beginning letter's sound. Then he places each card on the appropriate plate.

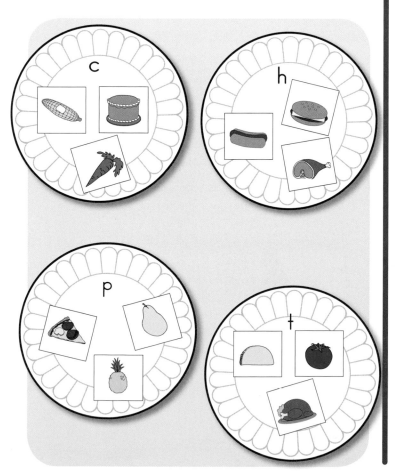

Build a Robot

Word families

Materials:
construction paper for each student:
   6" x 9" piece
   four 2" x 6" strips
   9" x 12" sheet
glue

A youngster decorates the 6" x 9" sheet of paper to make a robot face and labels it with a predetermined word family. She writes different words from the featured word family on the 9" x 12" sheet of paper and on each of the paper strips. Then she glues the pieces together so they resemble a robot.

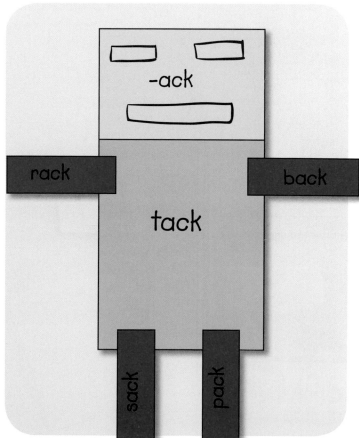

Stack and Spell

Spelling CVC words

Materials:
five clear plastic cups, labeled with consonants
    as shown
five opaque plastic cups, labeled with vowels
    as shown
blank paper

A child chooses a consonant cup and places it on top of a vowel cup so the vowel is between the consonants. If it spells a real word, he records it on his paper. He continues in the same manner with each of the remaining vowel cups. Then he repeats the process with each of the remaining consonant cups.

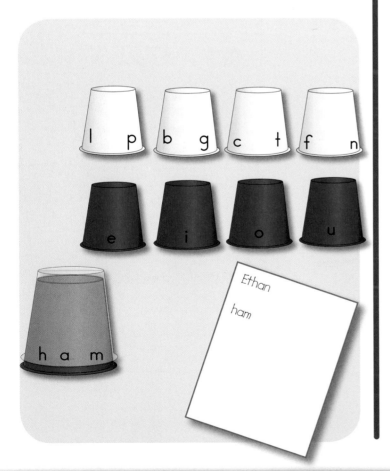

It's Raining Words!

Sorting words by category

Materials:
copy of page 86, cut apart
three puddle cutouts, labeled as shown
blank paper

A youngster sorts the cards by category above the appropriate puddles. Then she divides a sheet of paper into thirds and labels each section with one of the categories. She copies each group of words in the corresponding section of her paper.

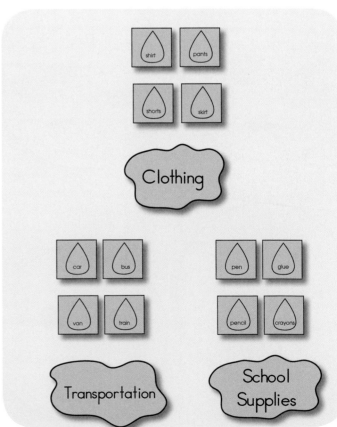

Rainbow Booklets

Alphabetical order

Materials:
colorful paper strips (five per child)
picture dictionary

A student finds five words in the picture dictionary and copies each on a different-colored paper strip. He mixes up the strips and then puts them in alphabetical order. When he is satisfied with the order of his strips, he stacks them in a neat pile in alphabetical order. At an appropriate time, he asks to have his stack of strips stapled along the side.

On a Roll

Word wall words

Materials:
die
blank paper

A child divides a sheet of paper into six columns and numbers the columns from 1 to 6. She rolls the die and finds a word on the word wall with the corresponding number of letters. If there are no words with the matching number of letters, she rolls again. Then she writes the word in the appropriate column on her paper. She continues in this manner as time allows.

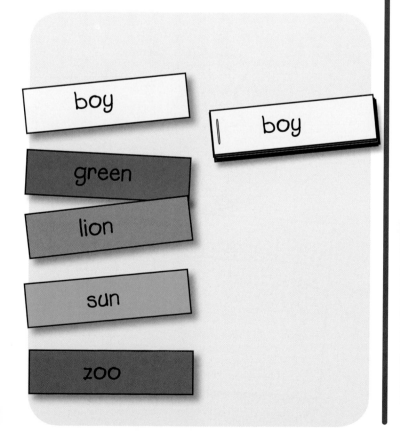

1	2	3	4	5	6
a	it an	the boy	girl then what	about these	number

Picture This

Beginning sounds

Materials:
letter manipulatives (consonants)
magazines
blank paper
scissors
glue
crayons

A student takes a letter and writes it at the top of his paper. Then he cuts out from magazines four pictures that begin with the selected letter and glues each one to his paper. If he cannot find four pictures, he draws a picture of an item beginning with the letter. The student repeats the activity with a different letter as time allows.

Caterpillar Parts

Writing sentences

Materials:
resealable plastic bags, each containing
    a set of circles programmed with
    words to make a sentence
construction paper caterpillar head
writing paper

A youngster places the head of the caterpillar on a flat surface. She removes the circles from a selected bag and reads each word. Then she arranges them behind the caterpillar's head in order to form a sentence. Next, she reads the sentence and copies it onto her paper. She returns those circles to the bag and repeats the activity by choosing a different bag of circles.

Chips and Dip

Punctuation

Materials:
potato chip cutouts labeled with
    statements and questions without
    the ending punctuation
empty potato chip canister or plastic bag
    for storing chip cutouts
2 plastic bowls labeled as shown
writing paper

A child takes a chip and reads the sentence. She places the chip in the bowl labeled with the correct ending punctuation. She continues in this manner until she has placed each chip in the appropriate bowl.

Setting the Scene

Literary response

Materials:
familiar picture book that includes multiple settings
6" x 9" strips of construction paper (one per child)
crayons

A student folds his strip into fourths and unfolds it. At the top of the first section, he writes the title and author of the book. In that section, he draws the first setting in the story. He continues drawing a different setting in each section of his paper, turning it over and continuing on the back if necessary. For an added challenge, the youngster labels each section with the name of the setting.

Box It!

Punctuation

Materials:
copy of page 87, cut apart
3 envelopes, programmed as shown (crayon boxes)

A youngster reads the sentence on a crayon, identifies the missing punctuation, and places the crayon in the corresponding crayon box. She continues in this manner until all the crayons have been sorted. For an added challenge, she writes on her paper a sentence with each punctuation mark.

Snapshots

Nouns

Materials:
blank paper
magazines
scissors
glue

A student labels each of three sheets of paper as shown. She cuts pictures of nouns from the magazines and glues them on the corresponding sheets. She continues to add pictures until each sheet has at least three objects represented.

Vocabulary Search

Sorting words by category

Materials:
construction paper (one sheet per child)
magazines
scissors
glue

A child folds his paper to create four sections and labels each section with a different category. Then he searches the magazine pages for pictures that fit each category. After he cuts out each picture, he glues it in the corresponding section. He continues in this manner until there are several pictures under each category.

One, Two, or Three?

Syllables

Materials:
3 cards labeled with the headings shown
word cards (words with one, two, or three syllables)

A student lays out the three heading cards to begin columns. For each word card, he reads the word and quietly claps to count the word parts. He then places the card under the corresponding heading. For an added challenge, the youngster writes one-, two-, and three-syllable words on three blank cards and adds them to the stack.

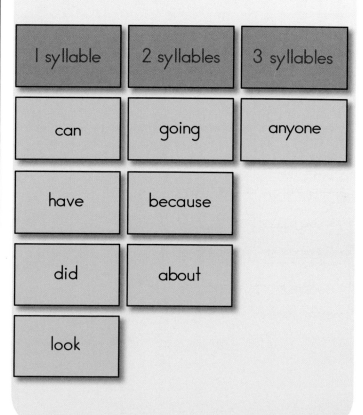

Sort It Out

Capitalization

Materials:
2 cards labeled with the headings shown
word cards with familiar words and
    proper nouns with no capital letters
blank paper

A student lays out the two heading cards to begin two columns. For each card, she determines whether the word should begin with a capital letter and then places it in the appropriate column. After she sorts all the cards, she labels a sheet of paper with the headings. Then she writes the words as she sorted them, adding capital letters where needed.

Capital	not capital
karen	park
november	run
tuesday	hill
dan	

Capital	not capital
Karen	park
November	run
Tuesday	hill
Dan	

Missing Middles

Short vowels

Materials:
cards labeled with CVC words with
    blanks for the vowels
blank paper

A child chooses a card and copies its partial word on his paper five times. He inserts a different vowel in each blank and reads his results. He then makes a check mark beside the real words. He selects another card and repeats the activity until he has used all the cards.

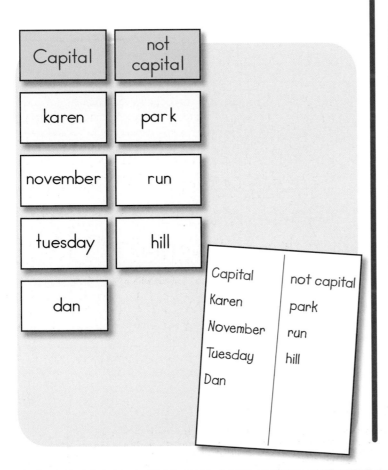

p_g

Barbara

✓ c<u>a</u>n   ✓ h<u>a</u>t   ✓ b<u>a</u>g
c<u>e</u>n   h<u>e</u>t   ✓ b<u>e</u>g
c<u>i</u>n   ✓ h<u>i</u>t   ✓ b<u>i</u>g
✓ c<u>o</u>n   ✓ h<u>o</u>t   ✓ b<u>o</u>g
c<u>u</u>n   ✓ h<u>u</u>t   ✓ b<u>u</u>g

p<u>a</u>g
✓ p<u>e</u>g
✓ p<u>i</u>g
p<u>o</u>g
✓ p<u>u</u>g

Mail Delivery

Word families

Materials:
envelopes, each programmed with a
    word family and containing several
    pieces of paper
letter tiles

A youngster selects an envelope and removes a sheet of paper. He tries different letter tiles at the beginning of the word family to form as many words as possible and lists each word on his paper. He then chooses another word family envelope and repeats the process.

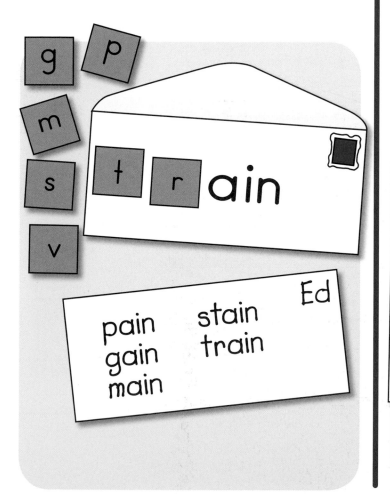

Alike and Different

Comparing characters

Materials:
student copies of page 88
2 familiar picture books
crayons

A student reviews the two books. On her paper she writes the book titles and draws a picture in each section of the main character from each story. She then writes how the characters from the two stories are alike and how they are different.

Roll a Letter

Initial consonants

Materials:
student copies of page 89, programmed
    with consonants
cube labeled with initial consonants from
    the recording sheet

A child rolls the cube and locates the letter on his recording sheet. Then he writes a word that begins with that letter in the bottom space above that letter. He continues rolling and writing until a column is full. For an added challenge, the student writes a sentence with one word from each column on the back of his paper.

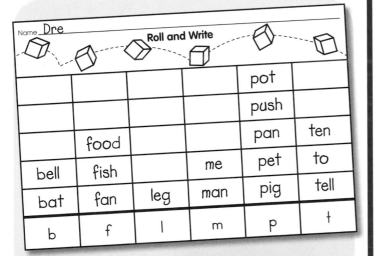

Clever Captions

Writing a caption

Materials:
postcard, photograph, or calendar picture, posted
paper strips (one per child)

A youngster looks at the picture. On a strip of paper, she writes a caption about the picture. She posts her caption under or beside the picture. For an added challenge, the child writes on a sheet of paper a story about the picture.

What's the Scoop?

Retelling a story

Materials:
ice cream scoop cutouts in a variety
    of light colors (three per child)
brown paper cones (one per child)
tape

A student recalls a story he has recently
read. He writes what happened at the beginning of the story on one scoop, what happened
in the middle of the story on another scoop, and
what happened at the end of the story on a third
scoop. He then writes the title of the book on a
cone. He tapes each scoop, in order, one atop
the other, and then attaches them to the cone.

Fancy Footwork!

Alphabetical order

Materials:
footprint cutouts programmed with
    words to be alphabetized
writing paper

A child reads the words on the footprint
cutouts. Then she selects the word that comes
first alphabetically and places it on the floor.
Next, she places the remaining footprints in
alphabetical order after the first footprint. Once
she has placed all the footprints, she writes the
words in order on her paper.

Reasons to Read

Purpose for reading

Materials:
student copies of the purpose-for-reading
   cards on page 90, cut apart and each
   group stacked separately
variety of fiction and nonfiction books

A youngster chooses a book to read, either for pleasure or to get information. After he reads the book, he writes about it on the appropriate card.

Reading for Pleasure

Title: Danny and the Dinosaur Author: Syd Hoff

I enjoyed this book because the dinosaur was real and went into the city with Danny.

Jared

Silly Sentences

Writing sentences

Materials:
4 cards, each labeled with a different adjective
4 cards, each labeled with a different plural noun
4 cards, each labeled with a different verb
blank paper
crayons

A student folds a sheet of paper to create four sections. She selects one card for each part of speech and arranges the cards to make a complete sentence. Then she writes the sentence in an empty section on her paper and illustrates it. She sets the cards aside and writes three additional sentences in the same manner.

Funny cats fly.

Funny   cats   fly

Leaping Frog

Initial consonants

Materials:
large pond cutout labeled with letters as shown
tagboard frog cutout (pattern on page 90)
blank paper

A child tosses the frog onto the pond and quietly names the letter the frog lands on or closest to. On his paper, he writes a word that begins with the corresponding letter. He continues in this manner as time allows.

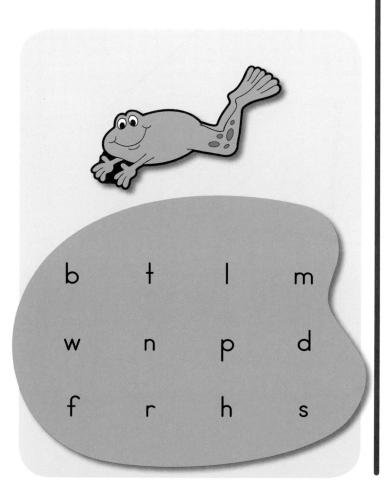

b   t   l   m

w   n   p   d

f   r   h   s

Read and Review

Literary response

Materials:
wordless picture book
list of questions similar to the ones shown
blank paper
crayons

A student reads the book. She writes its title and the author's name at the top of her paper. Then she chooses a question from the list, copies it on her paper, and answers it. When she is satisfied with her answer, she adds an illustration.

- What was your favorite part of the story?
- What was the main idea of the story?
- Tell about the beginning, middle, and end of the story.
- Did the story end like you thought it would? Why or why not?

Melissa
Pancakes for Breakfast
by Tomie dePaola

The Doctor Is In!

Editing sentences

Materials:
box of bandages
paper strips labeled with sentences needing
    corrections
writing paper

A child takes three strips. He copies each sentence onto his paper, correcting the mistakes. When he is satisfied with his work, he attaches a bandage to his paper to indicate that he has "healed" the sentences.

Story Flag

Cause and effect

Materials:
recently read book, with pages illustrating
    cause and effect marked
6" x 9" sheets of construction paper (one per child)
craft sticks (one per child)
tape
crayons

A student reviews an example of cause and effect in the story. She labels one side of her construction paper *Cause* and the other side *Effect.* Then she writes on the corresponding sides of the paper to describe the cause and effect. After she adds illustrations, she tapes the paper to a craft stick to make a flag.

Lots of Letters

Ending sounds

Materials:
copy of page 91, cut apart
letter tiles: *d, g, g, m, n, n, p, s, t, t*

A youngster names the picture on each card, stressing the ending sound. Then he matches each picture to its appropriate ending sound.

Category Cube

Writing a list

Materials:
cube labeled with categories
blank paper

A child rolls the cube and writes the category rolled at the top of a sheet of paper. Then he lists as many words in that category as he can. When he cannot think of any other words, he turns his paper over, rolls the cube again, and repeats the activity with a new category.

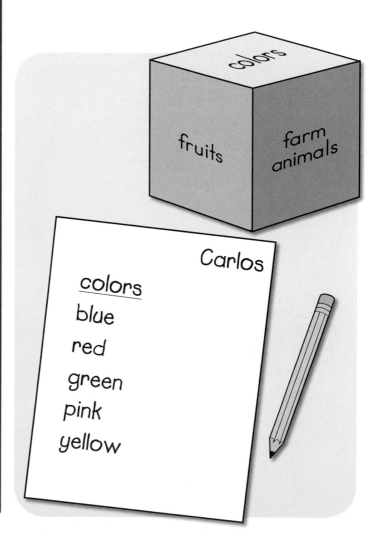

Tell All About It

Literary response

Materials:
student copies of page 92
several recently read books
crayons
scissors

A student selects a book and writes its title and author's name on the microphone handle. Then she writes about her favorite part of the story and adds an illustration. Next, she cuts out her microphone. For additional practice, she uses her microphone to retell the story to a classmate.

Spin a Word

Onsets and rimes

Materials:
2 spinners (pattern on page 90) prepared
    as shown, with one programmed
    with onsets and one programmed
    with rimes
highlighter
blank paper

A child spins the onset spinner and writes the corresponding onset on his paper. Then he spins the rime spinner. He writes the rime beside the onset to complete the word. (He may list a word more than one time.) If the word is a real word, he highlights it. If it is not a real word, he leaves the word unmarked. He continues in this manner as time allows.

Picture-Perfect Sentences

Nouns

Materials:
magazines
sentence strips
scissors
glue

A youngster cuts pictures of nouns from a magazine. Then she incorporates one or more of the pictured nouns into a sentence on a sentence strip. She continues writing sentences in this manner as time allows.

Meaty Middles

Segmenting words

Materials:
copy of page 91, colored and cut apart
2 laminated tan paper bread slices
laminated pink paper circle (meat)
wipe-off marker
paper towels

A student stacks the bread slices and meat to make a sandwich. She takes a card and quietly says the word aloud, stressing each sound. Next, she lays out her sandwich pieces and writes the beginning and ending letters on the bread slices and the middle letter on the meat. She reads the word aloud, tapping each letter as she says the corresponding sound. Then she wipes off the sandwich pieces and continues in the same manner with the remaining cards.

Give Me a Hand

Syllables

Materials:
12" x 18" sheets of construction paper (one per child)
magazines
scissors
glue

A child divides his paper into three columns. Then he traces his hand in each column, as shown. He numbers the handprints from 1 to 3. He finds magazine pictures of items that have one, two, or three syllables in their names and glues each picture in the appropriate column.

Alien Antics

Writing using an organizer

Materials:
student copies of page 93
writing paper
crayons

A student draws an alien in the spaceship on her organizer. She fills out the rest of the organizer to correspond with her illustration. Then she writes a short story about her alien, using the organizer as a guide.

Flowering Families

Word families

Materials:
copy of page 94, cut apart
4 flower cutouts, labeled as shown
blank paper

A youngster places each card on the flower labeled with the appropriate word family. Then she divides a sheet of paper into four columns and labels each column with a different word family. She writes the word for each picture in the corresponding column.

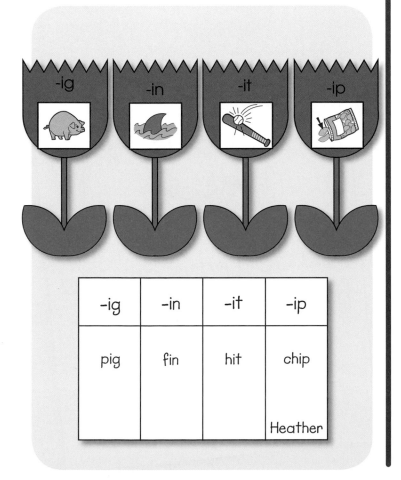

-ig	-in	-it	-ip
pig	fin	hit	chip
			Heather

A High-Flying Kite

Synonyms

Materials:
kite template
9" x 12" sheets of construction paper (one per child)
cards, each labeled with a different
    word from several synonym pairs
scissors
tape
yarn

A student traces the template on a sheet of construction paper and cuts it out to make a kite shape. He matches the cards to make synonym pairs and writes them on his kite. Then he tapes a length of yarn to his kite to make a tail.

chilly cold
little small
mad angry
happy glad
start begin

Ethan

Word Worms

Compound words

Materials:
green construction paper strips (five per child)
list of compound words
crayons
scissors

A student chooses five compound words from the list and writes each word on a paper strip. Then she rounds the corners of each strip and adds a face to make a worm. She cuts each worm so that each piece is labeled with half of the compound word. She scrambles the worm pieces and then matches them to make compound words.

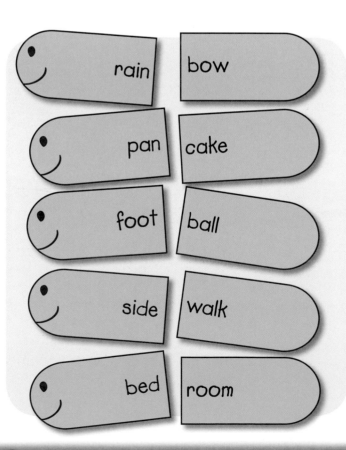

Words in Action

Verbs

Materials:
copy of the verb cards on page 95, cut apart
story paper
crayons

A child takes a verb card. He writes on a sheet of paper a sentence using the verb and then underlines the verb. Then he illustrates his sentence.

Three in a Row

Literary response

Materials:
student copies of the gameboard on page 96
familiar book
writing paper

A youngster selects a question on the gameboard, copies it on a sheet of paper, and answers it based on the book. After he answers the question, he colors it on his board. He answers two more questions in this manner, making sure to answer three questions in a row.

What is the setting?	Did you enjoy this book? Why?	Who are the main characters?
Why do you think the author wrote this book?	What is the title and who is the author of the book?	What is the main idea in the story?
What happened in the beginning, middle, and end of the story?	What was your favorite part of the story? Why?	Who is your favorite character? Why?

Picture Prompts

Writing ideas

Materials:
copy of the cards on page 97, cut apart and sorted into two containers that are labeled as shown
story paper

A student selects a picture from each container. Using the pictures as inspiration, she writes a brief story and then adds an illustration.

Characters   Settings

Rebekah

The girl is at the beach. It is hot, but she is dressed in winter clothes. She looks silly!

Monty the Monster

Short-vowel o

Materials:
student copies of page 80
lunch-size paper bag (one per student)
scissors
crayons

A youngster decorates the paper bag to make a monster. With assistance, she cuts a hole in the bag to make the monster's mouth. Then she cuts out her cards. For each card, she names the picture, stressing its vowel sound. If the picture has the short-vowel /o/ sound, she "feeds" it to her monster. If it does not, she sets it aside.

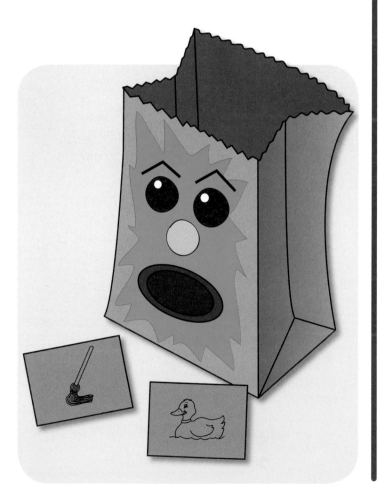

Days of the Week

Spelling

Materials:
cards labeled with the days of the week, each word cut into individual letters and stored in a separate resealable plastic bag
calendar
blank paper

A student arranges the letters in a bag to correctly spell a day of the week, referring to the calendar for help if needed. Then he copies the word onto his paper. He continues in this manner with the remaining bags. For an added challenge, he copies the words onto his paper in the appropriate order.

Fold, Write, and Draw

Singular and plural nouns

Materials:
copy of the noun cards on page 95, cut apart
blank paper
crayons

A student shuffles the cards and stacks them facedown. Then he folds his paper into four sections. He labels one side of his paper *singular* and the other side of his paper *plural.* For each card, he determines if the noun is singular or plural. He writes the noun in an empty section on the appropriate side of his paper and adds a corresponding illustration.

A Silly School

Identifying sentence subjects

Materials:
paper strips labeled with school-related
    people and items
paper strips labeled with sentence predicates
writing paper

A child pairs a strip labeled with a school-related person or item with a strip labeled with a predicate to make a sentence. She copies the sentence on her paper, circling the subject of the sentence. She continues in this manner with the remaining strips.

Mr. Hall

hugged a monster

Maria

The slide ate a bug.

Mr. Hall hugged a monster.

Story Mobiles

Main idea and details

Materials:
familiar book
sentence strips labled "Main Idea" (one per child)
blank cards labeled "Detail" (three per child)
hole puncher
yarn
scissors

A child writes the main idea of the book on the sentence strip and three details about the book on the blank cards. To assemble the mobile, she punches three holes in the sentence strip and a hole in each card. For each card, she cuts a length of yarn to tie it to the sentence strip.

Main Idea
Wendell was not a good house guest.

Detail:
When Sophie and Wendell played, Wendell made all the rules.

Detail:
At lunch, he painted with his peanut butter and jelly.

Detail:
He wrote his name on the bathroom mirror with toothpaste.

Stamp the Letter

Final consonants

Materials:
student copies of page 98
letter stampers
ink pad
scissors

A student cuts out the cards. She takes a card and says the name of the picture, stressing the final consonant sound. Then she stamps the appropriate consonant in the blank on the card. She repeats this process with each of the remaining cards.

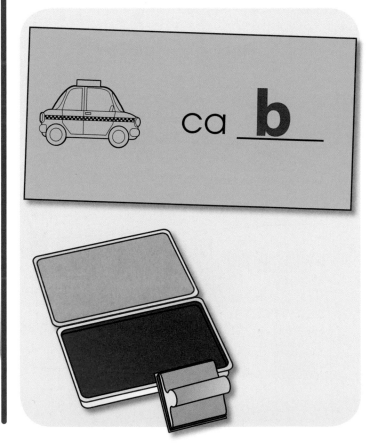

ca **b** ___

Colorful Words

Beginning blends

Materials:
cards labeled with words that begin with *bl* and *br*
blank paper
blue and brown markers

A youngster makes a T chart on blank paper and labels the columns as shown. He takes a card and determines whether the word's beginning blend is the same as *blue* or *brown.* Then he writes the word in the appropriate column using the corresponding marker. He continues in this manner with the remaining cards.

blue	brown
blank	branch
blow	bring
blink	brick

Eight Legs

Onsets and rimes

Materials:
black construction paper
red construction paper scraps
white crayon
scissors

A child uses the construction paper to make a spider. He uses the white crayon to write an assigned word family on the spider's body (see suggestions). Then he writes a different word from the word family on each of the spider's legs. For an added challenge, he writes on a sheet of paper sentences using the words.

Suggested Word Families:

-an	-ap
-at	-et
-ig	-in
-ot	-ug

Nifty Notebooks

Nouns

Materials:
copy of the cards on page 95, cut apart
4-page booklet (one for each child)
crayons

A youngster sorts the cards into two piles: nouns and not nouns. For each noun, she writes a sentence on a separate page of her booklet. Then she underlines the noun on each page and adds an illustration. Finally, she adds a title, such as "My Noun Notebook," to her booklet cover.

Two Make One

Compound words

Materials:
familiar books
blank cards
crayons

A child looks in a book to find a compound word that has two parts he can illustrate. He writes the compound word on a blank card and illustrates it. Then he folds the two ends of the card so that they meet in the middle. He writes each half of the compound word on a separate flap of the card. Finally, he illustrates each word on the corresponding flap.

Reasons to Write

Author's purpose

Materials:
student copies of the author's purpose
card on page 96
familiar book
crayons

A child writes the title of the book and the author's name on his card. Then he colors the appropriate face and writes to tell why he thinks the author wrote the book. After each child completes the activity, invite students to share their ideas with the group.

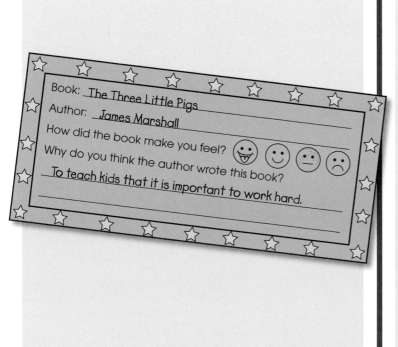

Pairing Up

Contractions

Materials:
large star cutout labeled as shown
blank paper

A youngster uses the words on the star to make five contractions and lists each contraction on her paper. For an added challenge, she writes a sentence using each contraction.

Vowel Booklet

Long vowels

Materials:
student copies of page 99
4" x 9" construction paper strips (six per child)
stapler
scissors
glue

A student cuts out the cards. She writes each vowel on a separate paper strip. Next, she glues each card to the strip labeled with the appropriate vowel. She stacks the strips and adds a cover strip with a title such as "My Long-Vowel Booklet." Then she staples the strips together along the side.

Putting It in Order

Writing organization

Materials:
4" x 6" blank cards (three per child)
6" x 18" construction paper strips (one per child)

A youngster writes the beginning, middle, and end of a story on separate blank cards. He mixes the cards and reads his story out of order to help him understand the importance of writing the details of a story in the correct order. Then he glues the cards in the correct order on the paper strip.

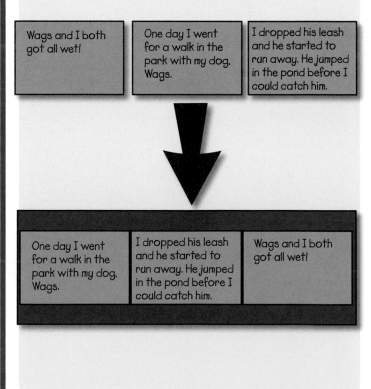

Wags and I both got all wet!

One day I went for a walk in the park with my dog, Wags.

I dropped his leash and he started to run away. He jumped in the pond before I could catch him.

One day I went for a walk in the park with my dog, Wags.

I dropped his leash and he started to run away. He jumped in the pond before I could catch him.

Wags and I both got all wet!

Change It

Short vowels

Materials:
student copies of a recording sheet with the
    left column programmed as shown
metal baking sheet
magnetic letters
blank paper

A child uses the magnetic letters to make a word from his paper on the cookie sheet. He quietly says the word, stressing its vowel sound. Then he replaces the middle letter with a different vowel and says the new word. If it's a real word, he writes it in an appropriate space on his recording sheet. If it is not a real word, he removes the vowel and tries a different one. He continues in this manner with the remaining words.

	Christian
hat	hot
map	mop
dog	dig
tin	tan
net	not
pig	

Scoop It Up!

Antonyms

Materials:
student copies of page 100
9" x 12" sheets of construction paper (one per child)
scissors
glue

A student cuts out the patterns. Then she matches each scoop to the cone labeled with its antonym. Next, she glues each antonym pair on a sheet of construction paper. For an added challenge, she writes each word of an antonym pair in a sentence.

Sorting Sticks

Synonyms

Materials:
4 plastic cups, labeled as shown
craft sticks labeled with synonyms
   of the words on the cups

A youngster reads the word on each craft stick and places it in the cup labeled with the synonym of the word. For an added challenge, she chooses a craft stick from each cup and uses each word in a sentence.

Scrambled Sentences

Subject-verb agreement

Materials:
4 blank cards, programmed with subjects
4 blank cards, programmed with predicates
writing paper

A child matches each subject to the appropriate predicate. Then he copies each sentence onto a sheet of paper. For an added challenge, he writes on the back of his paper an original sentence for each subject.

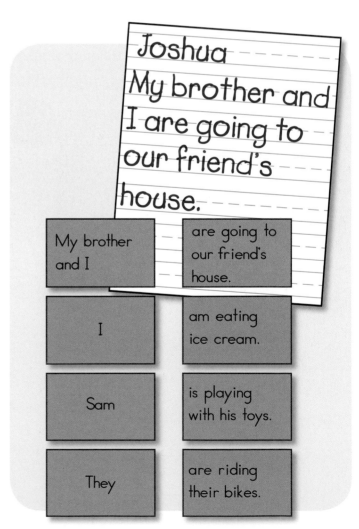

Vocabulary Wagons

Sorting words by category

Materials:
copies of page 101 (two per child)
cards programmed with different categories
construction paper
scissors
glue

A student chooses two category cards and labels each wagon wheel with one of the categories. In the spaces on each wheel, she writes a word from the corresponding category. Then she makes a construction paper wagon, cuts out her wheels, and glues them on the wagon.

Vocabulary Wagon

cucumber	pepper
carrot	Vegetables	celery
lettuce	onion

plum	apple
blueberry	Fruits	orange
pineapple	banana

Vegetables   Fruits

A New Egg

Writing a story

Materials:
12" x 18" sheets of construction paper (one per child)
scissors
crayons

A child folds a sheet of paper in half and cuts an egg shape through both thicknesses, leaving the fold intact. On the booklet cover, he draws a picture of a new animal that has hatched from an egg and writes the animal's name. Inside the booklet, he writes about the animal.

Tyson

Floposaurus

A floposaurus is a funny new animal. Its body is sort of flat. It has a long, flat beak. It likes to flop around to move. It is purple with green spots. It has huge ugly feet with long toes.

Toss, Read, and Write

Word families

Materials:
12-section muffin tin, each section
    labeled with a different word family
pom-pom
blank paper

A student tosses the pom-pom into the muffin tin. She reads the word family on which the pom-pom lands. Then she writes a word from the word family on her paper. She continues in this manner as time allows.

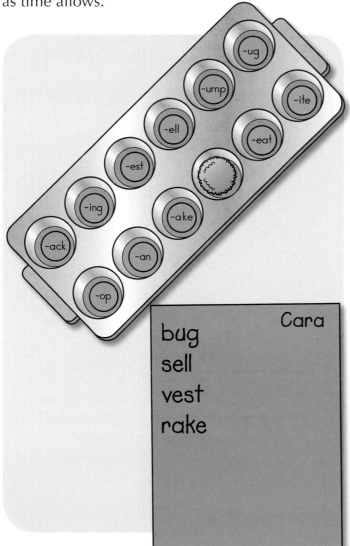

Cara

bug
sell
vest
rake

Word Hunt

Word wall words

Materials:
student copies of a reproducible similar
    to the one shown

A youngster reads a question or command from his paper. He uses the word wall to find the corresponding word(s) and then records each answer on his paper.

Name _Selassie_____

Word Hunt

1. What is the longest word
   on the word wall? _because___

2. What is the shortest word
   on the word wall? _I_____

3. Write five words that have
   three letters. _all, how, not, see, the_

4. Write five words that have
   four letters.
   been, came, down, into, what

5. Which words start with
   _wh_? _what, when, where, which, who_

6. Write four words with the long
   a sound. _came, day, made, make_

Ladybug Toss

Compound words

Materials:
leaf cutout labeled with parts of
    compound words as shown
2 red pom-poms
blank paper

A child tosses each pom-pom (ladybug) onto
the leaf cutout. He reads the words that the lady-
bugs are closest to and determines if they make
a compound word. If they do, he writes the word
on his paper. If they do not, he tosses the lady-
bugs again. For an added challenge, on the back
of his paper he lists, in alphabetical order, the
compound words he has made.

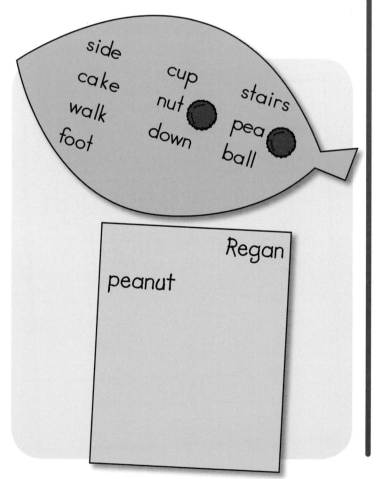

Follow the Rules

Plurals

Materials:
plural rules pattern on page 102
diecut shapes programmed with singular
    nouns (several shapes for each rule)
paper

A youngster reads the rules. Then she takes
a diecut shape and uses the appropriate rule to
write on her paper the plural form of the word.
She continues in this manner with the remaining
shapes.

Cover the Letters

Final consonants

Materials:
copy of the picture cards on page 102, cut apart
list of the letters shown
counters
blank paper

A child draws a 3 x 3 grid on his paper and labels each space with one of the listed letters. Then he shuffles the cards and stacks them face-down. He takes a card and places a counter on the grid space labeled with the ending letter of the pictured word. He continues in this manner until he has covered three letters in a row. Then he removes the counters, shuffles the cards, and plays another round.

Batter Up!

Writing sentences

Materials:
copy of page 103, cut apart and sorted into two stacks
writing paper

A student takes a ball card and a bat card. Then she writes a silly sentence using the resulting adjective-noun pair. She sets the pair aside and repeats the process as time allows.

Eating Cookies

Writing directions

Materials:
white paper circles (four per child)
black construction paper circles (two per child)
stapler
white crayon

A youngster writes on each of his white circles a different transition word (*first, next, then,* or *last*). Then, after each transition word, he completes a sentence explaining how to eat a chocolate sandwich cookie. He stacks his pages in order between the two black covers and staples them along the side. Finally, he uses a white crayon to write a title on the cover.

First, you twist the top cookie off.

How to Eat Sandwich Cookies by Tim

Roll and Respond

Literary response

Materials:
cube labeled with six questions from
    a copy of the gameboard on page 96
familiar book
writing paper

A student labels her paper with the book title. Then she rolls the cube and writes a response to the question she rolls. She repeats the activity until she has answered all six questions.

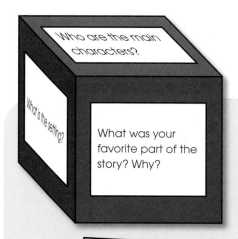

Who are the main characters?

What is the setting?

What was your favorite part of the story? Why?

Froggy's Day With Dad   Elise
1. The settings are inside Froggy's house and at the fun park.
2. The main characters are Froggy, his dad, and his mom.
3. My favorite part of the story was when Froggy went to play golf with his dad.

Roll a Blend

Beginning blends

Materials:
student copies of page 89, programmed with blends
cube labeled with blends

A child rolls the cube and names a word that begins with the blend rolled. She writes the word in the appropriate column of her sheet. She continues rolling and writing until a column is full. For an added challenge, the student writes a sentence with one word from each column on the back of her paper.

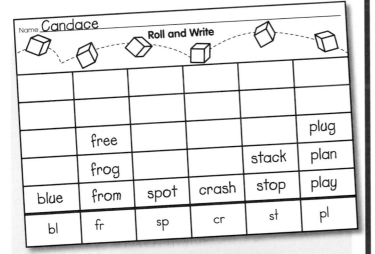

Let It Shine!

Verbs

Materials:
blank paper
crayons

A student writes the name of an animal in the center of her paper and draws a circle around it. Then she draws rays coming out from the circle. On each of the rays, she writes a different action verb describing something the animal can do. For an added challenge, the child writes sentences on the back of her sheet using the animal's name and some of the verbs she listed.

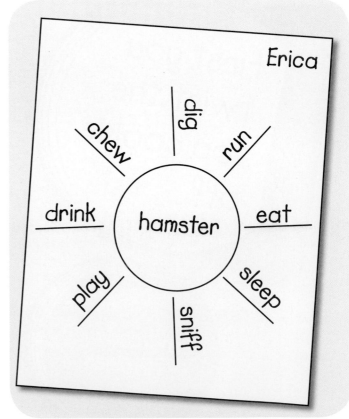

Apple Picking

Plurals

Materials:
copy of page 104, cut apart and
    placed in a basket
blank paper

A youngster takes a card from the basket and reads the word. If the word is a correct plural form, he places it in one pile. If it is incorrect, he places it in a different pile. After sorting all the cards, he folds his paper in half, unfolds it, and labels the columns as shown. He then writes the correct words under the smile and the incorrect words under the frown.

Puzzle Words

Writing a list

Materials:
2 large pictures mounted on tagboard,
    puzzle-cut, and labeled on the backs
    with words from 2 different categories
box lid
blank paper

A youngster mixes the two sets of puzzle pieces in a box lid. She removes each puzzle piece, reads the word on the back, and sorts the pieces into two topic-related piles. Next, she draws a line lengthwise down the center of her paper and lists the words from her two piles in the columns. To check her work, she assembles the puzzles picture-side up. For an added challenge, the student labels each list with the name of the category.

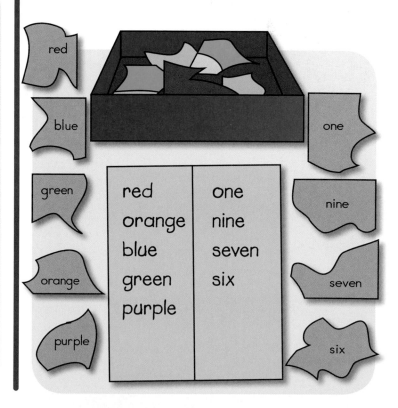

What's the Question?

Literary response

Materials:
bag containing the question cards
    on page 105, cut apart
familiar book
writing paper

A student rereads or reviews the book. He draws a question card from the bag and writes on his paper a question about the book beginning with that word. He then writes his answer to the question and repeats the process as time allows.

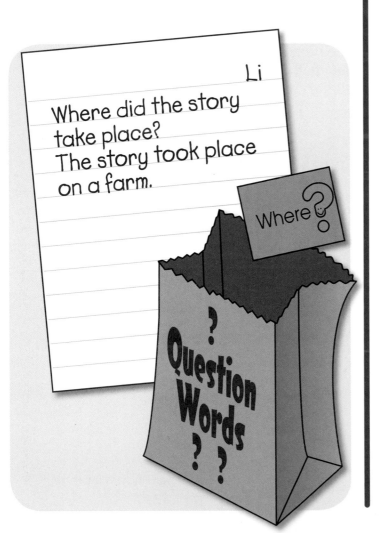

Brick by Brick

Hard and soft c and g

Materials:
student copies of page 106 (bricks)
12" x 18" sheets of white construction paper
    programmed as shown (one per child)
glue

A youngster cuts apart all the bricks, shuffles them, and stacks them facedown. Then she reads the word on a brick and places it in the corresponding section of her paper (wall). Once all the bricks are placed, she glues them to the wall.

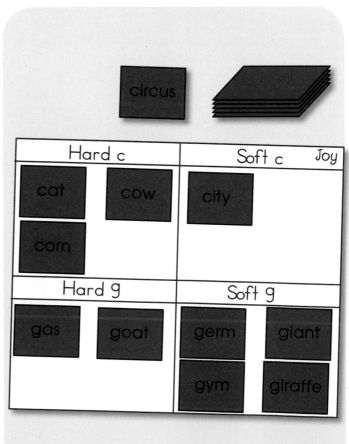

Word Search

Consonant digraphs

Materials:
9" x 12" sheets of construction paper (one per child)
magazines
scissors
glue

A child folds his paper into fourths, unfolds it, and labels the top of each section with a consonant digraph. He then cuts from a magazine several words containing each digraph. He underlines each digraph and glues each word to his paper in the corresponding section.

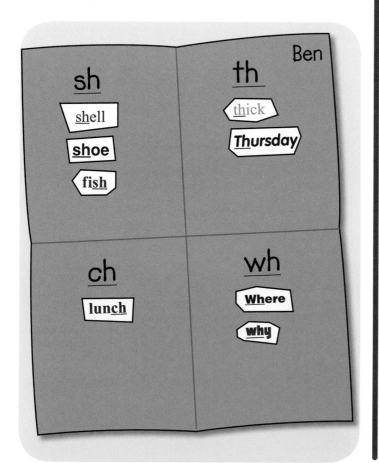

"Sense-ational" Writing

Adjectives

Materials:
cotton ball
marble
piece of sandpaper
blank paper
crayons

A student folds her paper into fourths, unfolds it, and labels the top of each section with the name of one of the displayed objects. The fourth section she titles with the name of a favorite snack. Below each noun she lists adjectives that describe how the object looks, sounds, feels, smells, or tastes.

cotton ball		marble	
fluffy	white	smooth	round
soft	quiet	blue	hard
			small

sandpaper		popcorn	
rough	thin	salty	yummy
scratchy	brown	white and yellow	
		crunchy	

What a Catch!

High-frequency words

Materials:
student copies of page 107, with the fish
    programmed with high-frequency words
paper clips
stick or pole with string and magnet attached
bucket
scissors
glue

A student cuts out the fish cards from her sheet. Then she attaches a paper clip to each one and places them in the bucket. She uses the fishing pole to catch a fish. After she reads the word, she glues it on her paper and writes a sentence. She continues in the same manner for each fish.

Name Sarita

What a Catch!

your — Today is your birthday!

like — I like cats.

they — They are nice.

Lid Toss

Long and short vowels

Materials:
large sheet of tagboard, labeled with long-
    and short-vowel words as shown
a supply of small plastic lids
blank paper

A youngster places the vowel poster on the floor. He labels his paper as shown. Then he tosses a lid onto a word and writes the word on the corresponding side of his paper. He continues in this manner until he has several words in each column.

face	coat	gift
dust	sea	bean
nose	deck	pond
hand	b○	kite
bake	cute	wish

	Dave
short vowel	long vowel
wish	face
bell	cute
	bean

Orange Grove

Nouns and verbs

Materials:
student copies of page 108
cards, each labeled with a noun or verb
crayons

A child reads the word on a card and writes it on the corresponding tree on her sheet. She continues in this manner until all the words have been read and written on a tree. Then she uses an orange crayon to draw and lightly color a circle around each word to complete her orange trees. For an added challenge, the youngster draws another tree on the back of her paper labeled "Adjectives." She writes four adjectives on that tree and circles them in orange.

Opposite Hopscotch

Antonyms

Materials:
small plastic lid
ten 5" x 7" cards labeled as shown
blank paper

A student folds his paper in half, unfolds it, and numbers it from one to ten. He lays the word cards out on the floor in a hopscotch pattern as shown. He tosses a lid at card number one. He writes the word beside number one on his paper, and writes its antonym across from it in the second column. He continues tossing and writing until he has landed on all ten words in order.

Cube Toss

Word families

Materials:
student copies of page 89, programmed
  with long-vowel word families
cube labeled with the same long-vowel
  word families

A student rolls the cube and writes a word
from that word family in the appropriate column
on her paper. She continues rolling and writing
until a column is full. For an added challenge,
the student writes a sentence with one word from
each column on the back of her paper.

Name Lisa	Roll and Write				
			right		
lake			night		
fake		meat	might		
cake		heat	light		
bake		beat	fright		
-ake	-ay	-eat	-ight	-one	-oat

Super Salad

Contractions

Materials:
2 paper plates labeled as shown
copy of the word cards on page 105, cut apart
blank paper

A youngster reads the word on a card. Then he
places the word card on the plate with the word
that can combine with it to form a contraction.
He writes the two words on his paper and then
writes the contraction they form. He continues
until he has sorted all the salad ingredients and
has written all the contractions.

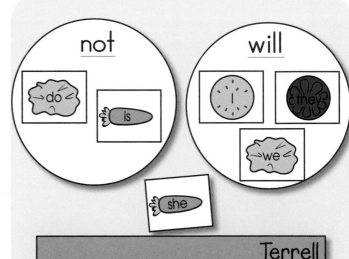

Terrell

1. do   not   don't
2. I   will   I'll
3. we   will   we'll
4. is   not   isn't
5. they   will   they'll

Find a Match

R-controlled vowels

Materials:
construction paper copy of page 109, cut apart
blank paper

A child shuffles the cards and lays them face-down in rows. He searches for a picture and the matching *r*-controlled vowel spelling by turning over two cards. If the two cards do not match, he turns them back over and flips over two new cards. When he locates a match, he removes the picture card, flips over the *r*-controlled vowel card, and continues playing until all cards have been removed.

Make the Connection

Cause and effect

Materials:
familiar book
5" lengths of yarn (one per child)
blank cards (two per child)
hole puncher

A student reviews the book. She selects an event from the story. At the top of a card, she writes "Effect" and underneath she describes the event. On another card, she writes "Cause" and describes what happened to cause that event. Then she punches a hole on the right side of the cause card and another hole on the left side of the effect card. She then ties a length of yarn to each of the holes to connect the cards.

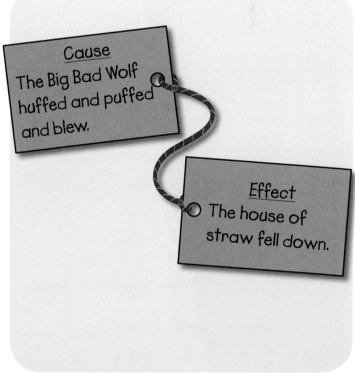

To Do

Writing a list

Materials:
cards, each labeled with a list idea and
    the number of words to list
half sheets of writing paper
stapler

A student takes a list card and writes its title on the top of a piece of paper. Then he numbers his paper accordingly and completes the list. He repeats the process until he has written several lists. Then he stacks the lists and staples them together at the top.

Spring Words
With Two Syllables

1.   flower
2.   garden
3.   sunshine
4.   rabbit
5.   April
6.   shower
7.   rainbow
8.   windy

10 types of
vehicles

5 shapes

8 spring words
with two syllables

Shape Up!

Facts from nonfiction

Materials:
large sheets of construction paper in a
    variety of colors (one per child)
nonfiction books students have read

A youngster trims a sheet of paper into a shape that represents a nonfiction book she has read. At the top of her shape, she writes the title of the book and the author's name. Then she lists three or more facts she learned from reading the book.

The Cloud Book
by Tomie dePaola
1. Clouds are drops of water or ice.
2. There are three main kinds of clouds.
3. Fog is a cloud that forms at ground
    level.

Susan

Clip and Check

Long and short vowels

Materials:
several wooden spring clothespins labeled
    with long- and short-vowel words
10" tagboard circle labeled as shown
writing paper

A child folds his paper in half, unfolds it, and titles each column as shown. He reads the word on a clothespin and clips the clothespin to either the "Long" or "Short" section of the circle. After he has clipped all the clothespins, he writes each word in the correct column on his paper and then removes each clothespin from the circle.

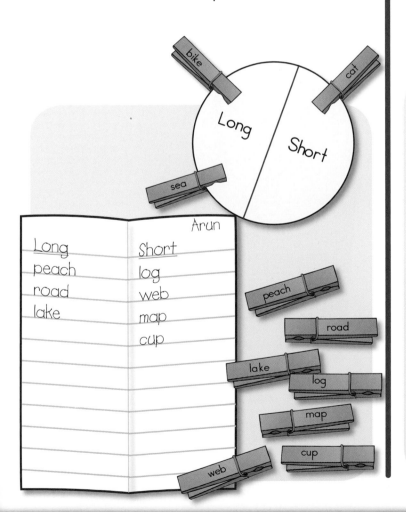

Zap!

High-frequency words

Materials:
craft sticks, each labeled with a high-frequency
    word as shown
craft stick labeled "Zap!"
cup

A student places all the sticks word-side down in the cup. She draws a stick and reads the word. If she is able to read the word, she keeps the stick. If she is unable to read the word, she replaces it and draws again. If she draws the "Zap!" stick, she must replace all her sticks and keep playing.

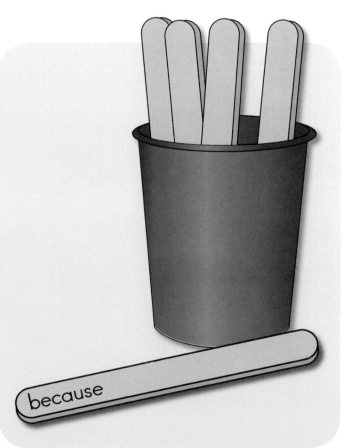

Poof! You're There!

Creative writing

Materials:
item to represent a magic lamp, such as a kettle,
     plastic teapot, or decorative plastic bottle
postcards or pictures of a travel destination
story paper
crayons

A child gently rubs the magic lamp and pretends he is magically transported to the featured destination. Using the pictures, he imagines himself having an adventure there. He rubs the magic lamp a second time for his return trip. Then he writes and illustrates a story about his adventure.

Shake and Choose

Consonant digraphs

Materials:
copy of page 110, cut apart
4 craft sticks, each programmed with a
     different digraph: *ch, sh, th,* and *wh*
cup

A student places the picture cards facedown in a pile and the sticks digraph-side down in the cup. Then she draws a card, names the picture, and determines the beginning digraph. Next, she gently shakes the cup and selects a stick. If the digraph on the stick matches the digraph the picture begins with, the child keeps the card. If it does not match, she returns the card to the bottom of the pile. Then she replaces the stick and continues playing.

Superstar *E*

Long-vowel words with silent e

Materials:
cards labeled with the following words:
    bit, can, cap, cub, cut, dim, fin, hid, hop,
    mad, not, pal, plan, rip, rob, rod, shin,
    tap, tub, us
small card labeled with an *e* surrounded
    by a star as shown
writing paper

A youngster reads a word card. Then she places the star card at the end of the word and reads the new long-vowel word. Next, she writes the pair of words on her paper. For an added challenge, the student writes three sentences on the back of her paper using three pairs of words from her paper.

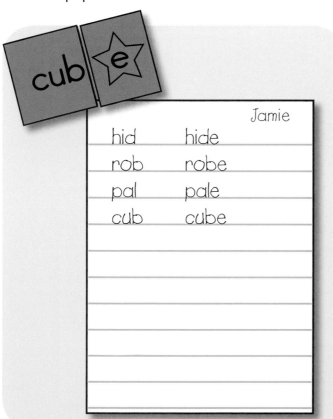

Happy Ending

Inflectional endings

Materials:
cards labeled with the following words:
    jump, laugh, look, play, sleep, talk, walk
large sheet of paper programmed as shown
beanbag
blank paper

A student places the construction paper on the floor and divides and labels his paper to match the construction paper. Then he takes a card and reads the word. Next, he gently tosses the beanbag onto the large paper and then writes the word from his card in the corresponding column on his paper, making sure to add the ending. He repeats the activity for each remaining card.

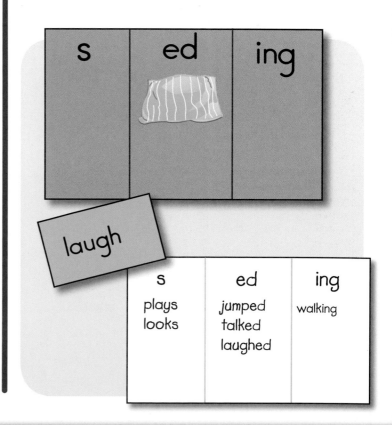

It's In the Bag

Alphabetical order

Materials:
die-cut shapes programmed with familiar words, placed in a bag that is labeled with the number of words to be alphabetized
writing paper

A student removes the designated number of cutouts from the bag. She arranges the cutouts in alphabetical order and then lists the sequenced words on her paper. She returns the cutouts to the bag and mixes them. Then she takes another selection of cutouts from the bag and uses them to write a second list.

5

Ruth Ellen
1. boat
2. doll
3. happy
4. lion
5. tent

That Extra Something

Adjectives

Materials:
cards, each programmed with a simple noun phrase
writing paper

A youngster selects a card and writes the phrase on his paper. Then he rewrites the phrase and adds a verb and one adjective to make a sentence. Next, he writes the sentence again, adding an additional adjective. He repeats the process one more time, adding one more adjective.

The tree

Andrew
The tree
The tree is green.
The big tree is green.
The big old tree is green.

Flip and Read

Parts of speech

Materials:
several familiar books
9" x 12" sheets of construction paper (one per child)

A child folds his paper in half and makes two cuts in the top half to form three flaps. He labels each flap with one of the following parts of speech: *Nouns, Verbs, Adjectives.* He looks through the books to locate nouns, verbs, and adjectives. Under each flap, he lists words belonging to each part of speech.

Pick a Stick

Generate questions about reading

Materials:
craft sticks programmed with the beginnings
    of questions, as shown
cup
familiar book
writing paper

A student places the sticks in a cup with the text-end down. After reading a book, she selects a stick from the cup and copies the question starter on her paper. She finishes the question, relating it to her story, and then writes its answer. She completes and answers more questions as time allows.

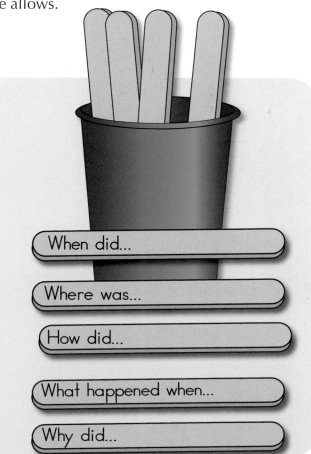

Special Delivery

Writing a letter

Materials:
empty box labeled "Mail"
letter-writing supplies
list of possible in-school mail recipients

A child uses the supplies to write a letter or postcard to a chosen student or staff member. She prepares the letter for delivery and places it in the mailbox. At a designated time, student mail carriers deliver the letters.

Pick a Pair

Contractions

Materials:
2 copies of the spinner on page 90, prepared and programmed as shown
writing paper

A student spins the two spinners and determines if the two words she lands on will form a contraction when combined. If they do, she records the two words and the contraction they form on her paper. If they do not, she chooses one of the spinners to spin again.

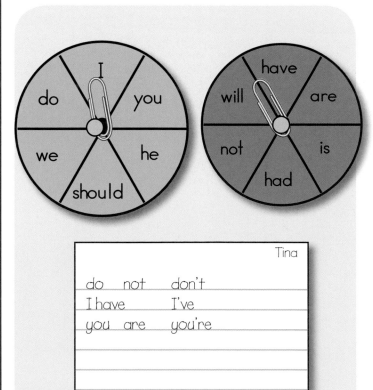

Choose a Pocket

Plurals

Materials:
pocket chart with cards programmed with
    plural rules as shown
cards, each programmed with a singular word to
    which one of the spelling rules applies
blank paper

A youngster folds his paper into four sections
and titles each section with a posted spelling
rule. He sorts each word card into the row that
shows the spelling pattern used to make the
word's plural form. He then writes the plural
form of each word in the corresponding section
of his paper.

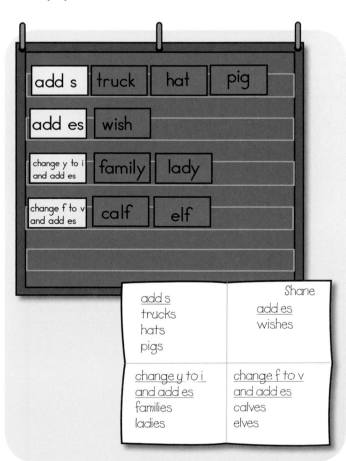

Make a Connection

Text-to-self connections

Materials:
familiar book
blank paper

A student reviews the book and then folds his
paper in half. On the first half, he writes about
something from the book that reminds him of
himself. On the second half, he writes about the
connection between the story and his own life
experiences. Then he illustrates each section.

She didn't eat the cold porridge.

I don't like it when my oatmeal gets cold.

Picture Cards
Use with "Tap, Tap, Tap" on page 7.

Word Cards
Use with "Truck Stop" on page 7.

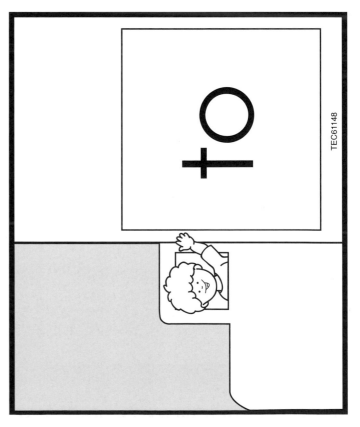

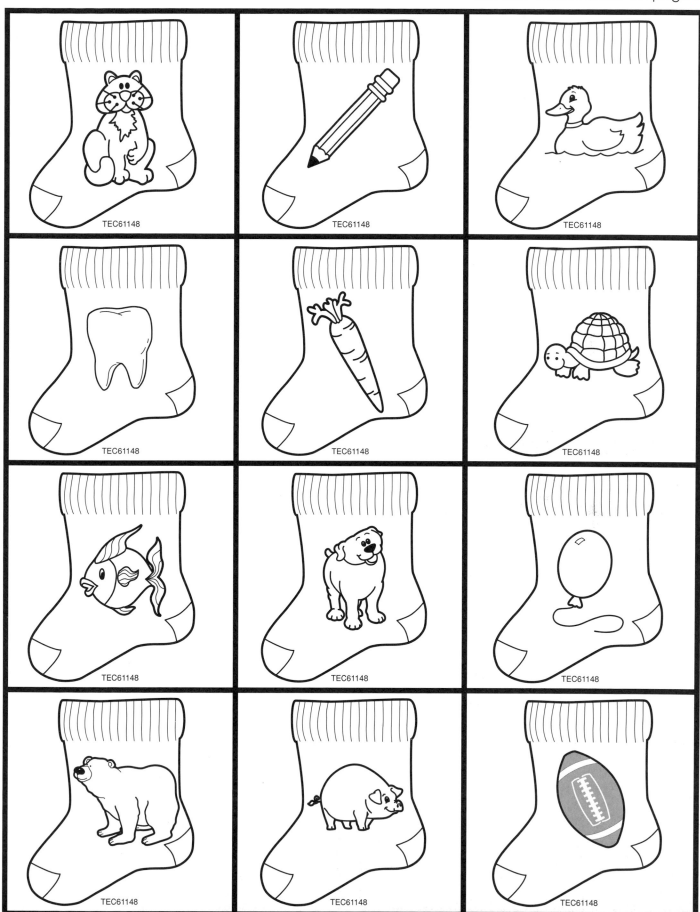

TEC61148

TEC61148

TEC61148

TEC61148

TEC61148

TEC61148

TEC61148

TEC61148

TEC61148

TEC61148

TEC61148

TEC61148

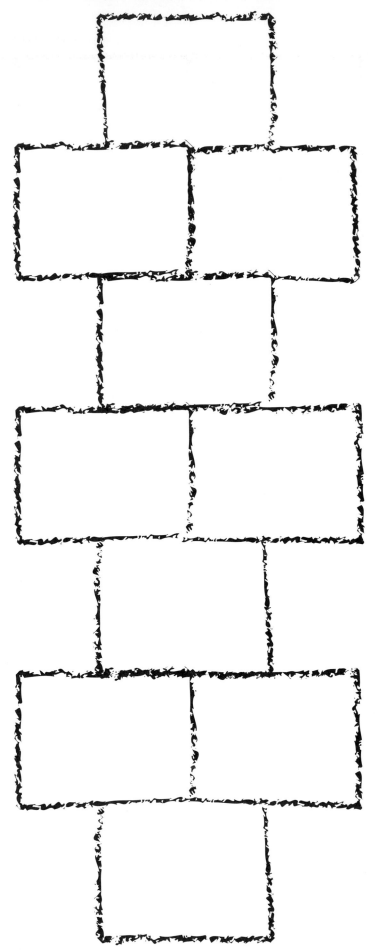

Super Simple Independent Practice: Language Arts • ©The Mailbox® Books • TEC61148

78 **Note to the teacher:** Use with "Hopscotch Fun" on page 11.

lip	rip	car	jar
cat	hat	dog	log
fox	box	cone	bone

TEC61148

Picture Cards

Use with "Say and Sort" on page 16 and "Monty the Monster" on page 46.

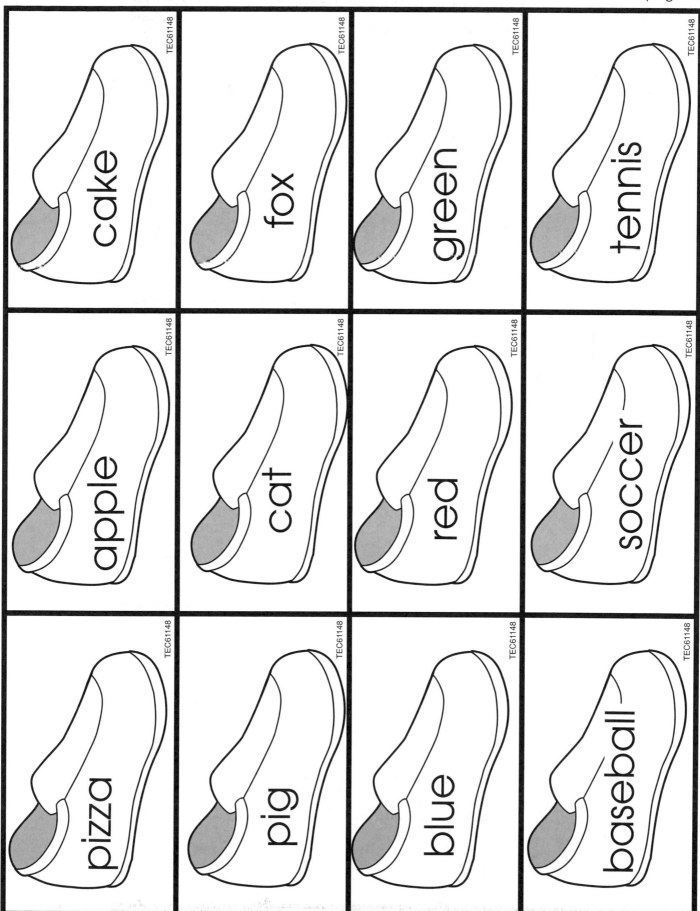

cake

fox

green

tennis

apple

cat

red

soccer

pizza

pig

blue

baseball

Vowel Spinner
Use with "Making Words" on page 19 and "Spin a Vowel" on page 23.

TEC61148

Sentence Starter Strips
Use with "Simple Story" on page 13.

One day,	1
Then	2
Next,	3
Finally,	4

TEC61148

cat

TEC61148

well

TEC61148

frog

TEC61148

cake

TEC61148

bug

TEC61148

Reality and Fantasy Cards

Use with "Could It Happen?" on page 24.

TEC61148

TEC61148

TEC61148

TEC61148

TEC61148

TEC61148

TEC61148

TEC61148

TEC61148

TEC61148

TEC61148

TEC61148

TEC61148

TEC61148

TEC61148

TEC61148

TEC61148

TEC61148

TEC61148

TEC61148

Word Cards
Use with "It's Raining Words!" on page 26.

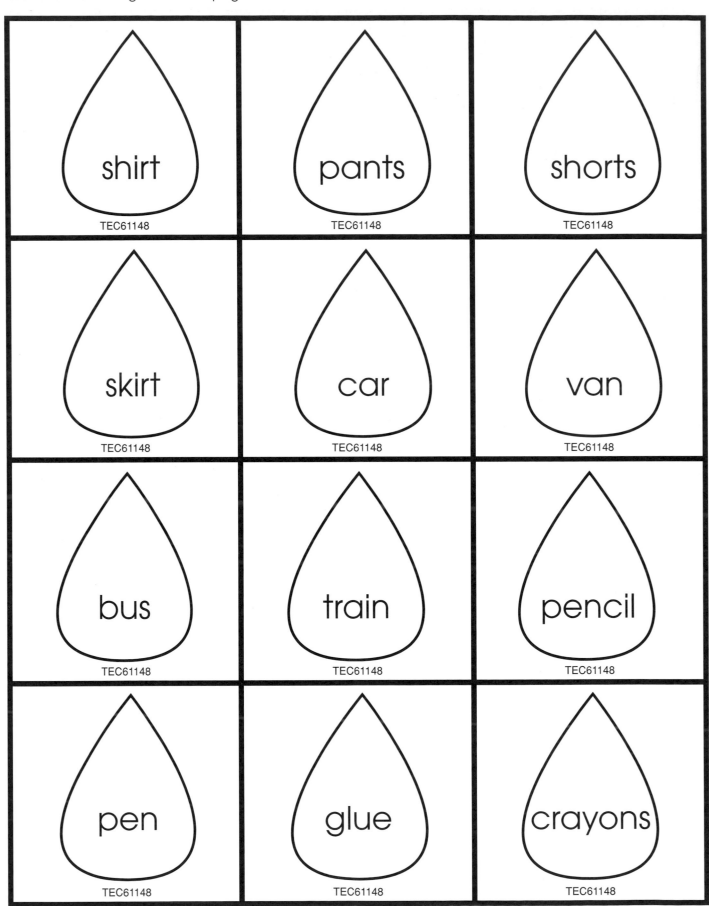

shirt

TEC61148

pants

TEC61148

shorts

TEC61148

skirt

TEC61148

car

TEC61148

van

TEC61148

bus

TEC61148

train

TEC61148

pencil

TEC61148

pen

TEC61148

glue

TEC61148

crayons

TEC61148

The girl sang a song

TEC61148

Walk with me to the store

TEC61148

Where is your book

TEC61148

Will you help me

EC61148

How long will you be gone

TEC61148

Hooray, I just won a prize

TEC61148

Hey, watch out for that car

TE 61148

I ate an apple

TEC61148

A pig rolled in the mud

TEC61148

My cat sleeps all day

TEC61148

Can you ride a bike

TEC61148

What is your name

TEC61148

Wow, that is a big spider

TEC61148

Oh boy, we are going to the zoo

TEC61148

Alike and Different

Name _____

Book title: _____

Book title: _____

The main characters in the stories are alike because _____

_____

They are different because _____

_____

Super Simple Independent Practice: Language Arts • ©The Mailbox® Books • TEC61148

Note to the teacher: Use with "Alike and Different" on page 33.

Name _____

Roll and Write

Super Simple Independent Practice: Language Arts • ©The Mailbox® Books • TEC61148

Note to the teacher: Use with "Roll a Letter" on page 34, "Roll a Blend" on page 60, and "Cube Toss" on page 66.

Purpose-for-Reading Cards
Use with "Reasons to Read" on page 36.

Reading for Pleasure

Title: _____ Author: _____

I enjoyed this book because _____

_____

_____

TEC61148

Reading for Information

Title: _____ Author: _____

When I read this book, I learned _____

_____

_____

TEC61148

Frog Pattern
Use with "Leaping Frog" on page 37.

TEC61148

Spinner Pattern
Use with "Spin a Word" on page 40 and "Pick a Pair" on page 74.

TEC61148

Super Simple Independent Practice: Language Arts • ©The Mailbox® Books • TEC61148

Picture Cards

Use with "Lots of Letters" on page 39 and "Meaty Middles" on page 41.

TEC61148

TEC61148

TEC61148

TEC61148

TEC61148

TEC61148

TEC61148

TEC61148

TEC61148

TEC61148

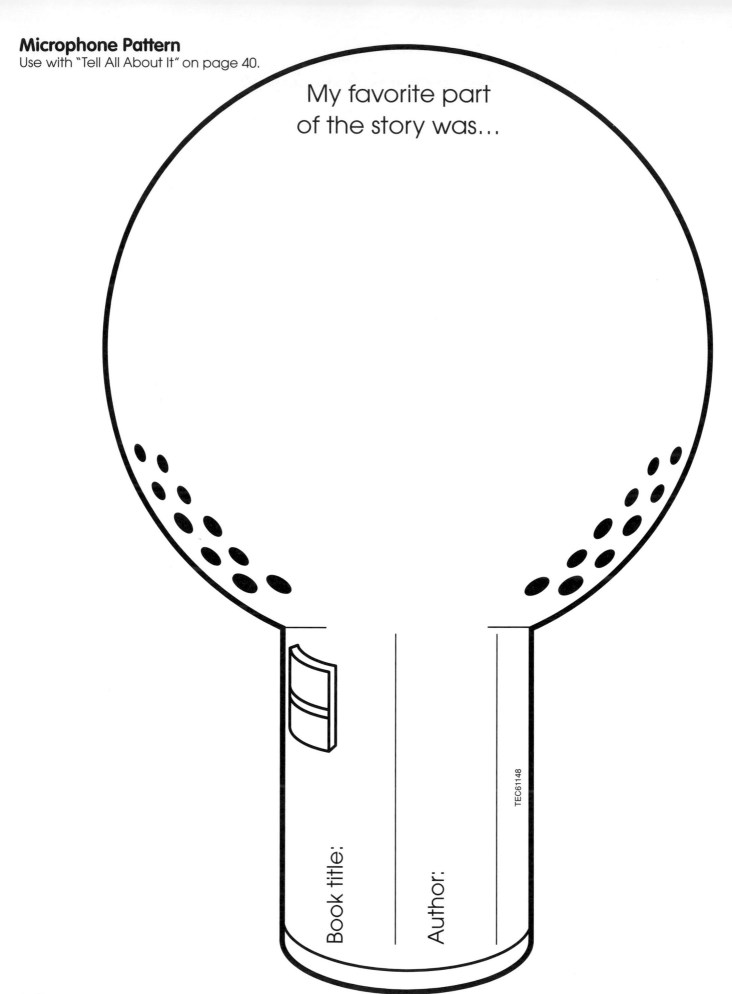

My favorite part
of the story was...

Book title:

Author:

TEC61148

Name _____

All About My Alien

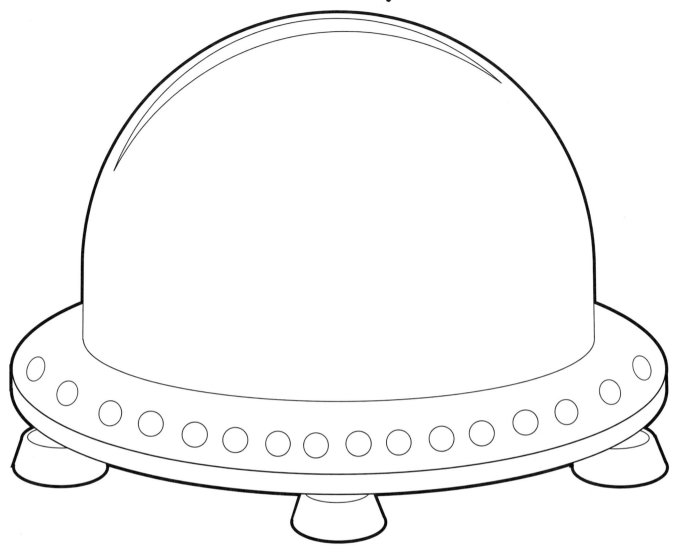

My alien's name is _____ .

It looks like _____

_____ .

It likes to _____

_____ .

Note to the teacher: Use with "Alien Antics" on page 42.

Picture Cards
Use with "Flowering Families" on page 43.

TEC61148

TEC61148

TEC61148

TEC61148

TEC61148

TEC61148

TEC61148

TEC61148

TEC61148

TEC61148

TEC61148

TEC61148

Super Simple Independent Practice: Language Arts • ©The Mailbox® Books • TEC61148

runs	sings	laughs	jumps
TEC61148	TEC61148	TEC61148	TEC61148
hops	skips	eats	writes
TEC61148	TEC61148	TEC61148	TEC61148

Noun Cards
Use with "Fold, Write, and Draw" on page 47 and "Nifty Notebooks" on page 50.

pig	tree	cat	cup
TEC61148	TEC61148	TEC61148	TEC61148
frogs	books	blocks	flowers
TEC61148	TEC61148	TEC61148	TEC61148

Gameboard Pattern

Use with "Three in a Row" on page 45 and "Roll and Respond" on page 59.

What is the setting?	Did you enjoy this book? Why?	Who are the main characters?
Why do you think the author wrote this book?	What is the title and who is the author of the book?	What is the main idea in the story?
What happened in the beginning, middle, and end of the story?	What was your favorite part of the story? Why?	Who is your favorite character? Why?

Super Simple Independent Practice: Language Arts • ©The Mailbox® Books • TEC61148

Author's Purpose Card

Use with "Reasons to Write" on page 51.

Book: _____

Author: _____

How did the book make you feel? 😛 🙂 😐 🙁

Why do you think the author wrote this book?

_____

_____

TEC61148

TEC61148

TEC61148

TEC61148

TEC61148

TEC61148

TEC61148

TEC61148

TEC61148

TEC61148

TEC61148

GROCERY STORE

TEC61148

HOSPITAL

TEC61148

TEC61148

TEC61148

ABC

TEC61148

Picture Cards

Use with "Stamp the Letter" on page 48.

ca _____ TEC61148	mo _____ TEC61148
ba _____ TEC61148	fa _____ TEC61148
lea _____ TEC61148	dru _____ TEC61148
fla _____ TEC61148	boo _____ TEC61148
bea _____ TEC61148	bu _____ TEC61148

TEC61148

TEC61148

TEC61148

TEC61148

TEC61148

TEC61148

TEC61148

TEC61148

TEC61148

TEC61148

TEC61148

TEC61148

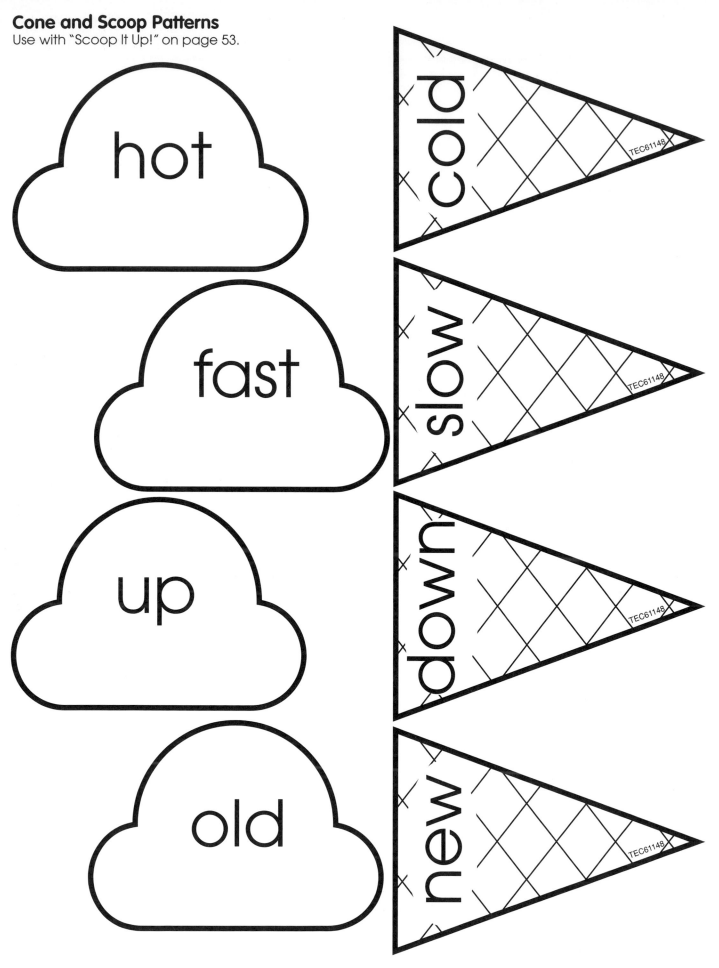

hot

cold

fast

slow

up

down

old

new

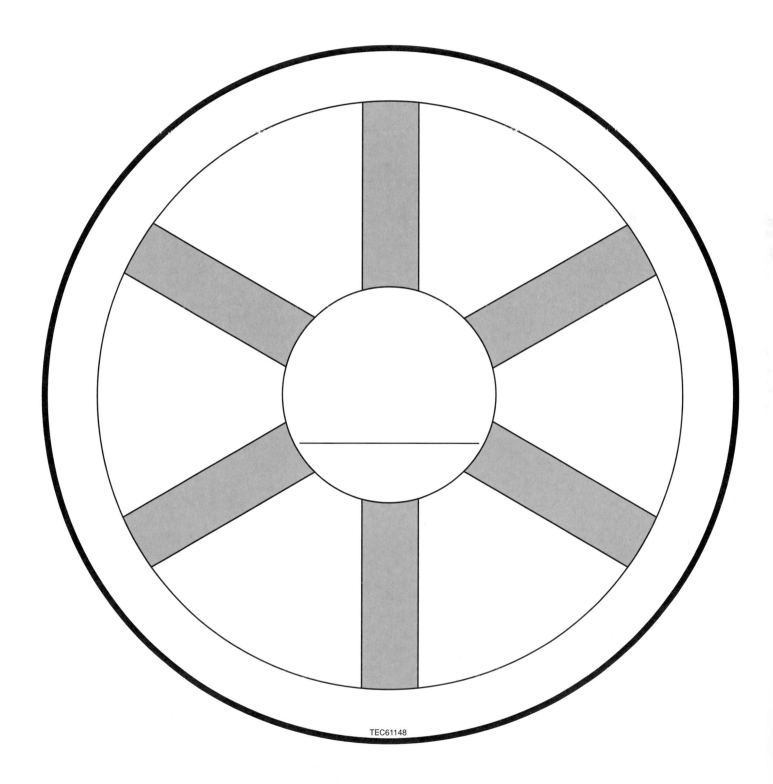

TEC61148

Plural Rules Pattern
Use with "Follow the Rules" on page 57.

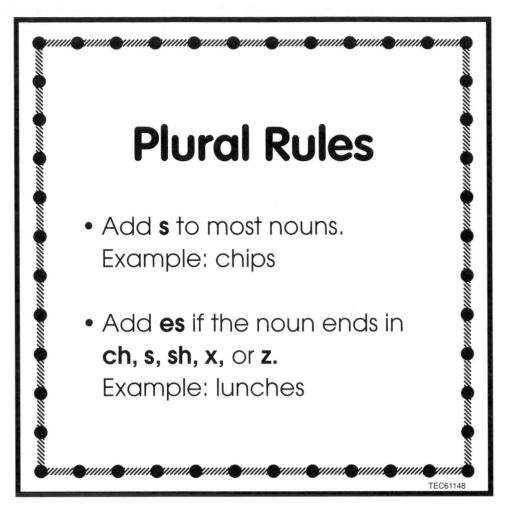

Plural Rules

- Add **s** to most nouns.
  Example: chips

- Add **es** if the noun ends in
  ch, s, sh, x, or **z.**
  Example: lunches

TEC61148

Picture Cards
Use with "Cover the Letters" on page 58.

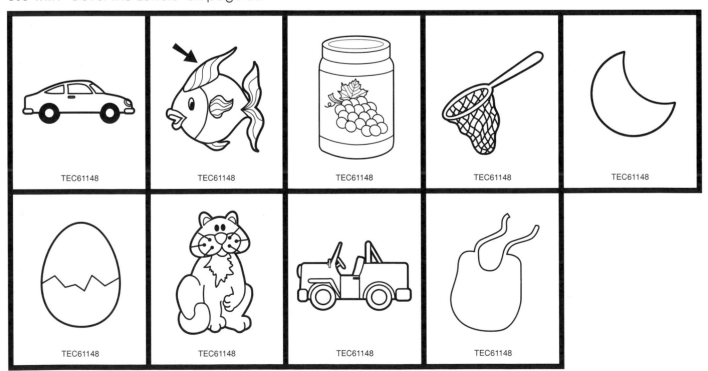

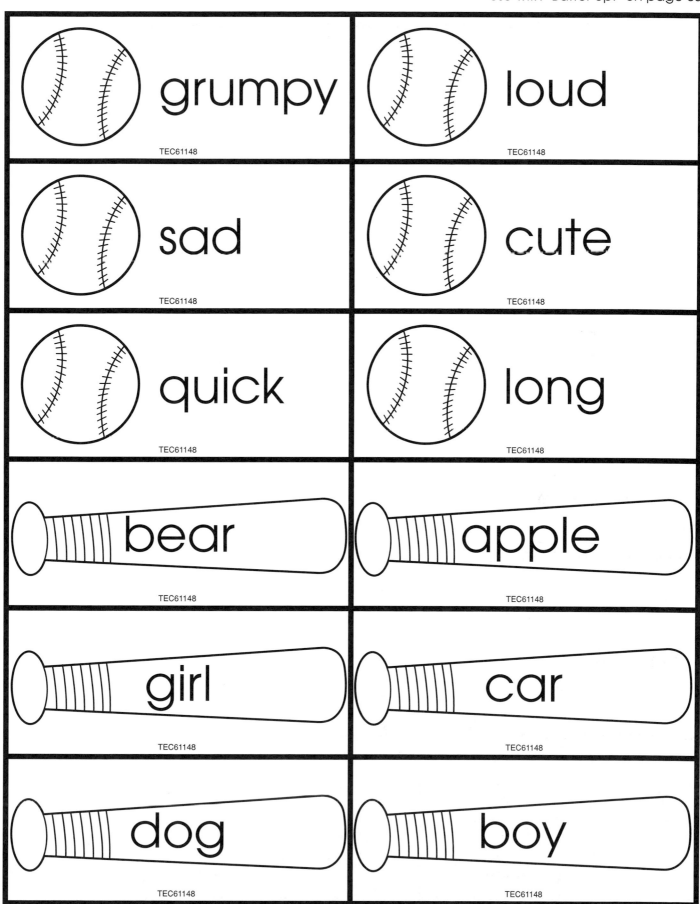

grumpy

TEC61148

loud

TEC61148

sad

TEC61148

cute

TEC61148

quick

TEC61148

long

TEC61148

bear

TEC61148

apple

TEC61148

girl

TEC61148

car

TEC61148

dog

TEC61148

boy

TEC61148

Word Cards

Use with "Apple Picking" on page 61.

birdes	foxs	childs	doges
lunches	cars	foots	wishs
cats	trees	men	dishes
pencils	mice	cards	boxes

Super Simple Independent Practice: Language Arts • ©The Mailbox® Books • TEC61148

Question Cards
Use with "What's the Question?"
on page 62.

Word Cards
Use with "Super Salad" on page 66.

Who? TEC61148

What? TEC61148

When? TEC61148

Where? TEC61148

Why? TEC61148

should TEC61148

they TEC61148

would TEC61148

I TEC61148

is TEC61148

she TEC61148

do TEC61148

he TEC61148

have TEC61148

we TEC61148

Super Simple Independent Practice: Language Arts • ©The Mailbox® Books • TEC61148

gym TEC61148	gum TEC61148	cent TEC61148	corn TEC61148
giraffe TEC61148	game TEC61148	circus TEC61148	cat TEC61148
germ TEC61148	gas TEC61148	city TEC61148	cow TEC61148
giant TEC61148	goat TEC61148	circle TEC61148	cup TEC61148

Name _____

What a Catch!

Super Simple Independent Practice: Language Arts • ©The Mailbox® Books • TEC61148

Note to the teacher: Use with "What a Catch!" on page 64.

Name _____

108

Nouns

Verbs

Note to the teacher: Use with "Orange Grove" on page 65.

ur			
	TEC61148	TEC61148	TEC61148

or			
	TEC61148	TEC61148	TEC61148

ir			
	TEC61148	TEC61148	TEC61148

er			
	TEC61148	TEC61148	TEC61148

ar			
	TEC61148	TEC61148	TEC61148

Picture Cards

Use with "Shake and Choose" on page 70.

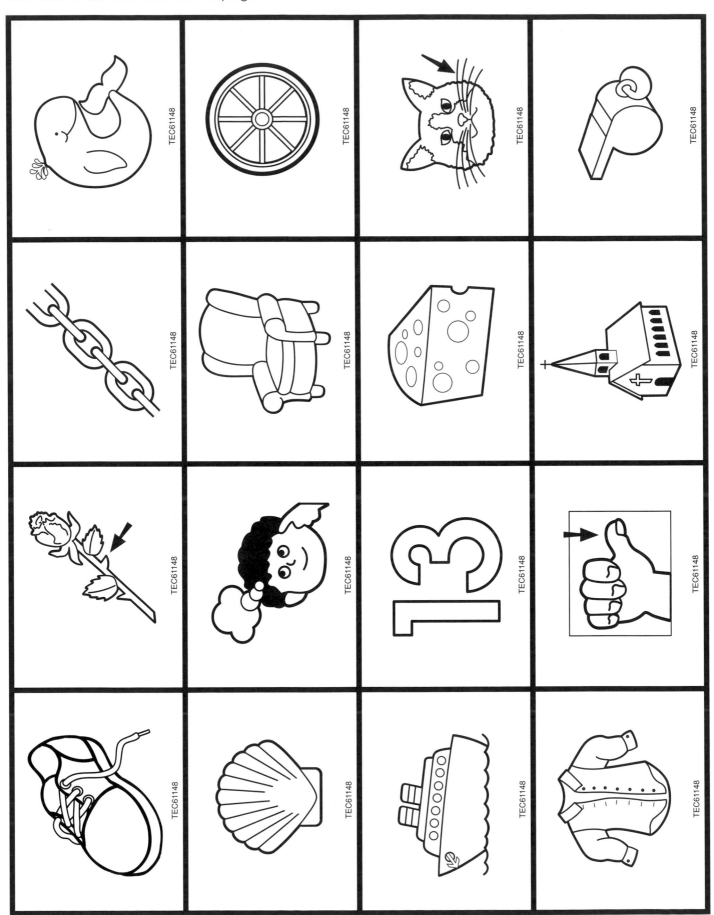

Super Simple Independent Practice: Language Arts • ©The Mailbox® Books • TEC61148

Skills Index

Language Conventions

capitalization, 9, 16, 32

editing sentences, 38

identifying sentence subjects, 47

parts of speech

   adjectives, 63, 72

   nouns, 13, 30, 41, 47, 50

   nouns and verbs, 65

   nouns, verbs, and adjectives, 73

   verbs, 44, 60

punctuation, 18, 29, 30

subject-verb agreement, 54

Phonemic Awareness and Phonics

beginning blends, 49, 60

beginning sounds, 5, 9, 11, 28

consonant digraphs, 63, 70

ending sounds, 39

final consonants, 48, 58

hard and soft *c* and *g,* 62

initial consonants, 14, 20, 25, 34, 37

making words, 21

onsets and rimes, 40, 49

rhyming, 12, 20

segmenting words, 41

spelling

   CVC words, 19, 26

   names, 5

   words, 15, 19, 46

vowels

   identification, 12

   long, 52, 71

   long and short, 64, 69

   r-controlled, 67

   short, 16, 23, 32, 46, 53

word families, 6, 10, 14, 25, 33, 43, 56, 66

Reading Comprehension and Literary Response

author's purpose, 51

cause and effect, 38, 67

characters

   analysis, 24

   comparing, 33

facts from nonfiction, 68

fantasy and reality, 24

generate questions about reading, 73

literary response, 29, 37, 40, 45, 59, 62

main idea and details, 48

making predictions, 21

purpose for reading, 36

stories

   recalling, 22

   retelling, 35

text-to-self connections, 75

Word Skills and Vocabulary

alphabetical order, 4, 27, 35, 72

antonyms, 53, 65

compound words, 44, 50, 57

contractions, 51, 66, 74

high-frequency words, 7, 11, 17, 18, 23, 64, 69

inflectional endings, 71

plurals, 47, 57, 61, 75

sorting words by category, 10, 17, 26, 31, 55

syllables, 7, 31, 42

synonyms, 43, 54

word wall words, 27, 56

Writing

caption, 34

creative, 22, 70

descriptive, 15

directions, 59

ideas, 45

letter, 74

letter formation, 4, 8

list, 39, 61, 68

organization, 52

sentences, 6, 8, 28, 36, 58

story, 13, 55

using an organizer, 42